The Ext
Have Been (

On June 20, 1992, Sarah Martin was awakened from a very strange dream, a dream totally unlike any other she'd ever had. "I was in a white room with . . . things. I can't remember their faces. I just remember talking to them, and I was in a white room. And they were talking to me. This is what they said: 'Why are you so involved in this [presidential] campaign? Why are you wasting your time? It's going to fall apart, one by one, and whoever wins, it doesn't matter because the whole system is going to come down around everybody. And there's going to be a rebellion. And you're not a part of this, so don't get involved.'"

Once Sarah had awakened, she was stunned to see a large object hovering outside her bedroom window. The object was covered with brightly colored lights and made a low buzzing noise.

Sarah was also struck by the sudden and total lack of animal noises outside while the UFO was present. Not one cricket made a noise.

But what concerned Sarah most of all was the well-being of her unborn baby. She was originally pregnant with twins; however, one of the fetuses died in utero. Sarah's doctor told her the chances of carrying the other child to full term were approximately one in five million.

Could the UFOs in Topanga Canyon have had something to do with Sarah's difficult pregnancy?

About the Author

Preston Dennett (California) is a field investigator for the Mutual UFO Network (MUFON). He has more than fifty articles published in most of the major UFO publications and is the author of *UFO Healings* and *One in Forty: The UFO Epidemic.* He has worked with the television programs *Sightings, National Geographic Explorer,* and *Encounters.*

To Write to the Author

If you wish to contact the author or would like more information about this book, please write to the author in care of Llewellyn Worldwide and we will forward your request. Both the author and publisher appreciate hearing from you and learning of your enjoyment of this book and how it has helped you. Llewellyn Worldwide cannot guarantee that every letter written to the author can be answered, but all will be forwarded. Please write to:

Preston Dennett
℅ Llewellyn Worldwide
P.O. Box 64383, Dept. K221-6
St. Paul, MN 55164-0383, U.S.A.

Please enclose a self-addressed stamped envelope for reply, or $1.00 to cover costs. If outside U.S.A., enclose international postal reply coupon.

Eyewitness Accounts of the California Sightings

UFOs

over

Topanga

Canyon

Preston Dennett

1999
Llewellyn Publications
St. Paul, Minnesota 55164-0383 U.S.A.

FIRST EDITION
First Printing, 1999

Cover design: Lisa Novak
Cover photo: Lee Rhoads
Book design and editing: Michael Maupin

Library of Congress Cataloging-in-Publication Data

Dennett, Preston E., 1965–
UFOs over Topanga Canyon : eyewitness accounts of the California sightings / Preston Dennett.—1st ed.
p. cm.
Includes bibliographical references and index.
ISBN 1-56718-221-6 (trade paper)
1. Unidentified flying objects—Sightings and encounters—California—Topanga State Park. I. Title.
TL789.5.C2D46 1999
001.942′09794′93—dc21
99-17974 CIP

Llewellyn Publications
A Division of Llewellyn Worldwide, Ltd.
P.O. Box 64383, Dept. K221-6
St. Paul, MN 55164-0383, U.S.A.

Printed in the United States of America

Contents

Author's Note

No BOOK IS possible without the assistance of a great number of people. First, I would like to give special thanks to Colin Penno and the staff of the *Messenger*, the Santa Monica Mountains News and Arts Publication. Without their influence, the Topanga Canyon encounters might never have become known.

I would also like to thank all the witnesses and their families whose accounts appear in this book. Bravely facing possible ridicule and disbelief, they still allowed their stories to be told. Without them this book would never have been written. The names of some of the various witnesses have been changed and pseudonyms were used to protect their privacy. Some of the witnesses who agreed to use their names appeared in the Topanga *Messenger* articles from January, 1989 to May, 1995.

I would also like to thank the Malibu/Lost Hills Police Department for their help in my investigations.

Finally I would like to thank Christine "Kesara" Dennett for her invaluable assistance during one of the most extensive UFO cases I've ever investigated.

Introduction

WHEN I FIRST began investigating unidentified flying objects in 1986, I had no idea that I was living directly in the center of a UFO hotspot.

Topanga Canyon is a small community of about eight thousand people in the Santa Monica Mountains west of Los Angeles. Unlike most cities in Los Angeles County, it is still amazingly rural. There are no sidewalks, no traffic signals and very few street lights.

It is a very close-knit community and many of the residents know each other. There is an annual country fair complete with a bake-off, a watermelon-seed-spitting contest and a tug-of-war contest over a large mud puddle. With an approximate size of fifty square miles, real-estate development remains strictly controlled. New houses can only be constructed on large lots so that the natural beauty largely remains preserved.

The geology is typical of southern California. Topanga Canyon (not to be confused with nearby Tujunga Canyon, which has also had its share of UFO encounters) is narrow and winding, with steep mountains rising as high as three-thousand feet. The hillsides are thick with buckwheat, sage, ceanothus, chaparral, sumac, poison oak, and wildflowers of all sorts. Eucalyptus, oak, and sycamore trees crowd the moist creek-beds, while the mountaintops are studded with huge out-croppings of bedrock and sandstone. One two-lane boulevard, Highway 27, divides the canyon.

Topanga Canyon is also the home of Topanga State Park, which holds the title of the second-largest inner-city park in the entire world. Wildlife in the area continue to flourish. It is not unusual to see cougars, deer, coyotes, fox, rabbits, and raccoons roaming the landscape.

It was the ideal place for a child to grow up. I spent many summers camping out in the natural sandstone caves, building forts, climbing trees, tromping through the creek collecting tadpoles.

I never once thought about UFOs.

Then, in 1986, after reading several books about UFOs, I became curious about the phenomenon. Although the books were very convincing, I still found it hard to believe that extraterrestrials were actually visiting our planet. So I was determined to conduct my own mini-investigation. I began asking everyone I knew, "Do you believe in UFOs? Have you ever seen one?" To my surprise, several people responded positively. People I had known for years were now telling me that not only did they believe in UFOs, they had seen them.

That was the beginning of the end of my skepticism. I could no longer deny the fact that something was flying around our skies. No more could I bask in the comfort of my own doubt. I no longer had that luxury.

So I continued to interview my friends who had seen UFOs, and I wrote a short article for the local Topanga newspaper, the *Messenger*. Shortly after submitting the article, Colin Penno, the editor-in-chief, telephoned me praising the article. It would be in the next issue.

Unfortunately, the results of the article's publication were somewhat disappointing. I received only three calls: one from a man who believed in UFOs, one from a man who once saw a UFO documentary, and one from a lady who dreamed about a UFO. Otherwise, there was very little response. This was the first time the *Messenger* had ever printed a UFO story, and it seemed it would be the last.

In fact, over two years passed without incident. I assumed that there were no more sightings in Topanga and kept myself busy with other cases in the Los Angeles area. Then, in June 1992, Colin Penno called with some remarkable news. There was a massive UFO wave occurring over Topanga. The police were receiving multiple calls, and so was the office of the *Messenger*. One event led to another, and I soon found myself embroiled in a huge investigation.

Using standard investigative techniques such tracking down and interviewing witnesses, coordinating with the police, networking with other investigators, researching previously published UFO reports and more, I quickly uncovered literally hundreds of reports from Topanga Canyon alone, and dozens of others from neighboring Santa Monica and Malibu. These included virtually every type of report including unexplained lights, metallic ships, landings, car chases, helicopter chases, missing-time abductions, healing cases, animal mutilations, strange creatures, and possible government surveillance. The large number of reports shocked me and I realized Topanga must be a UFO hotspot similar to Gulf Breeze,

Florida, or Hudson Valley, New York. In fact, the similarities were so striking that I decided to do a comparative study of well-known UFO hotspots to see how Topanga Canyon fit in.

I knew of other hotspots or flap areas besides Gulf Breeze and Hudson Valley. For example, Exeter, New Hampshire had experienced a remarkable UFO wave in the late 1960s, and Wytheville, Virginia was also a famous UFO hotspot. Fyffe, Alabama and the San Luis Valley in Colorado were two other locations that had earned a reputation for high levels of unexplained UFO activity. Using these six locations, I discovered that there were ten signs of a UFO flap area. Each of the five areas has at least eight of the following ten qualifications:

1. *A Full Range of UFO Encounters.* A flap area should have reports that include all types of encounters including sightings of unexplained lights, metallic ships, beams of light from objects, entity contact, landing-trace cases, animal evidence, and missing-time abductions.

2. *An Extremely Large Number of UFO Encounters.* Depending on the size and population of the area, there should be anywhere from a hundred to a thousand or more UFO reports.

3. *A Long History of UFO Encounters.* There should be some evidence that sightings have been occurring in the area for many years, even decades.

4. *Predictable Encounters and UFO Watchers.* In UFO flap areas, encounters happen with

such consistency that they can be predicted. This consistency brings in floods of people hoping to actually see a UFO.

5. *Independent Witnesses to the Same UFO Encounter.* In UFO flap areas, the UFOs seem to have little or no fear of being seen, and in fact, seem to "put on displays." A single object is often seen by large numbers of people in different locations.

6. *Involvement of Official Agencies.* In every UFO flap area, official agencies such as police, Navy, Air Force, Coast Guard, fire department and others become embroiled in the controversy as they try to deal with the flood of reports. In some cases, United States Federal agencies also become involved.

7. *Recorded Encounters in Local Newspapers.* In flap areas, encounters are so numerous that they simply cannot be ignored. Sooner or later, the controversy surfaces in local newspapers.

8. *Books Written About Encounters.* In most cases, UFO flap areas generate huge public interest, which again, sooner or later, results in the publication of a book.

9. *Sightings by Investigators.* A UFO flap area has such a high level of activity that those who investigate the area often end up having their own sightings.

10. *Photographs Taken of UFOs.* Again, UFO flap areas have such a high level of activity that, sooner or later witnesses are able to photograph the objects. In several cases, film and video are also taken.

Of course, a UFO wave could still be present without exhibiting all ten qualifications. However, the chances are good that if a major flap area does exist in a certain area, most of the above qualifications will be present. The more qualifications present, the higher the probability is that a UFO flap area exists.

Some ufologists have pointed out the possibility that a UFO wave might be more of a social phenomenon than anything else. This is because a single publicized UFO incident provokes other reports, creating a "snowball effect." Potentially, any area could become a flap area or produce a UFO wave, given the right impetus.

Whether or not this is true is hard to say. However, if UFO flaps are indeed a social phenomenon, why aren't there more areas that have gained such a reputation? With so much interest in UFOs, there should be flap areas in every state. And yet, the number of well-known flap areas can be counted on one hand.

Regardless of how they start, a UFO wave is a very real phenomenon. Hundreds of encounters are reported and the entire community is suddenly thrust into an enigmatic and entirely public situation. The issue becomes the focus of controversy as people try to deal with the confusing possibilities of mysterious visitors from outer space and a government cover-up.

When I first started investigating UFOs over Topanga, none of the ten qualifications for a UFO flap was apparent. There were only a few isolated sightings, although these sightings were quite dramatic. After over three years of intense investigation, I concluded that Topanga fulfilled all ten of the qualifications of a UFO flap area.

This book is the story of that investigation.

1

The First Encounters

IT WASN'T UNTIL 1986 that Topanga residents began to share their UFO encounters with me. Friends shared stories that they hadn't dared to tell anybody else for fear of ridicule and disbelief. These were normal, sincere people talking about things that they themselves didn't understand. They pleaded for answers. *Why Topanga?*

At first all I could do was record their stories and reassure them that others were having similar experiences. At the time, I had no idea that Topanga was a UFO hotspot. Although I marveled at the incredible coincidence of having friends and neighbors who had seen UFOs, I simply assumed that these sightings were isolated events. Actually, they represented the tip of the iceberg. They were also to mark the beginning of a long and extensive investigation.

Sylvia Walters, who lives on Saddlepeak—one of the highest points in Topanga—was the first Topanga resident to share her story. Walters is the only person I know who is licensed to travel in the air, on land, and in water. She is not only a scuba-diver, but also a pilot and flight instructor. She has lived in Topanga most of her life and is very familiar with the air traffic.

It was around 10:00 P.M. during the summer of 1974 that Sylvia and a friend had an encounter with an unidentified flying object. What is interesting about this sighting is that it also involved sound. Sylvia and her friend were alerted by a strange, low humming noise. Sylvia relates that it happened when she was fourteen years old.

"My friend and I were in my room and we heard this humming noise. We looked outside and there was a very bright, oval-shaped light that seemed to be float-ing and moving down, and going over . . . not over, but it went down behind the ridge . . . It was a yellowish light. It was oval."

Sylvia thought the object was strange even though the sighting lasted only seconds. "Probably for about four or five seconds, all in all. I mean, at the time, it seemed a lot longer. But looking back on it, it was something that—we looked out and it was like it moved across maybe about five degrees through the horizon before it went down behind the ridge . . . It was moving fairly slowly. My friend thought it was a meteorite . . . And I said, 'Oh, okay. That's what it was.'"

Like many UFO eyewitnesses, Sylvia had difficulty estimating the size and distance of the object. She said it could have been close and small, or far away and large. She watched it go behind a nearby ridge, and estimates that it was probably a fairly large object, about one or two miles away. It was apparently about the shape of a half-moon.

At first Sylvia agreed that the object was probably a meteorite. It wasn't until afterwards that she began to question that assumption. After all, the object was moving very slowly and had a distinctly defined oval shape. It also made a humming noise. As she said, "It was like a steady rumble or hum, kind of a low dial tone . . ."

When asked if the experience scared her at all, Sylvia replied, "No, it didn't. At the time I was saying, 'Wow, that's a UFO!' And my friend said, 'No, no, no, it's not a UFO. It's a meteorite.' So we both went back to bed. But no, I wasn't scared. It didn't seem anything to be scared about."

It should be clear that the object seen by Sylvia and her friend was no meteorite. The description doesn't even come close to a plane, helicopter, or other conventional aircraft. It couldn't have been a planet, star, ball-lightning, or a fireball. None of these explanations match all the details of shape, size, sound, brightness, color and movement of the object.

If it wasn't any of these, then what *was* it?

Taken alone, Sylvia's encounter would be a mere curiosity. However, soon after Sylvia's disclosure of her sighting, I learned of another sighting.

This sighting turned out to contain levels of mystery that have yet to be revealed. It occurred within a few miles of the other encounters, on the northern edge of Topanga Canyon along Mulholland Drive.

Mark Grant works as the manager of a tow-truck company and lives in an apartment in the San Fernando Valley. He agreed to tell me his story though he admitted it frightened him a little. In fact, he told nobody about what he saw for years afterward.

Grant's experience occurred on Mulholland, a dirt road that runs along the northern rim of Topanga Canyon. Although the road itself is somewhat isolated with no houses for miles, the San Fernando Valley spreads out below in panoramic view. Most of west Los Angeles is visible from the road. At night, the view is spectacular.

One night in 1982, at around 1:00 A.M., Grant and a friend were driving along Mulholland when they decided to pull off the road and look at the view. As they sat on the hood of the car admiring the city lights, their attention was caught by a triangular formation of lights that moved across the sky above them. About halfway across the sky, the lights stopped and hovered.

As Grant recalled, "We were both looking out towards the sky and saw some lights. And it was very strange because they were in a triangular pattern. We observed the lights for, I'd say, maybe fifteen minutes or so. We had been talking about it, looking at these lights, and we thought they were maybe helicopters or something like that.

"About fifteen minutes after we first observed [the lights], they started coming towards us, and they split off in three directions. The triangular pattern was sort of two on the bottom and one on top. And the one on top kind of looked like it was going up and away and towards us all at the same time. And the two at the bottom looked like they went straight at us, around our periphery. And at the same time, they looked like they were going away too. They just kind of disappeared.

"There were colors when they were moving. And as they were steady, they were very bright, but like a white light."

4

Before the lights swooped down toward them, Grant had a distinct feeling that they were watching him. The feeling became stronger and stronger until the objects swooped down toward them. Only then did they flash into bright colors. As Grant recalled, "Well, it was a very bright fluorescent green and sort of bright orangish-red, and a very, very deep but bright blue, from left to right, on bottom to top, in that order. And they kind of changed colors as they moved. They seemed like they changed colors, almost streaked. I guess because they were moving so fast or whatever. They could have been lines of light or just moving so fast I couldn't catch it with my eye. I guess that's why they were going towards us and away from us at the same time."

They heard no noise from the objects, nor could they tell how close the objects were, or what was their size. Grant said that they looked like large car headlights, but he felt that the objects were actually much larger.

After the objects disappeared, both witnesses were stunned and speechless. They didn't even discuss the event among themselves, and immediately drove home.

Later, Grant dreamed that it was really just an object suspended on a cable from a helicopter. Still, the incident left him with a vague sense of fear. Like many UFO eyewitnesses, Grant and his friend kept their sighting a secret. Before they had laughed at people who claimed to have seen UFOs. Now Grant wasn't laughing.

After investigating his sighting, I had a feeling something was missing. I had Grant go over the encounter again, but somehow, something just didn't seem right. It wasn't until a few years later that I re-examined Grant's account and realized why the incident seemed unresolved.

The most curious feature of Grant's experience is that the objects seemed to be swooping toward and away from them at the same time. Then there was the fact that the encounter scared both of them badly, and that they felt they were being observed.

Only later did I learn what these details might mean. In ufology, there is a phenomenon known as a "missing-time encounter." Many people experience a lapse of time in conjunction with a close-up UFO encounter. Abduction researchers have discovered that missing time can be almost seamless, with very few clues of the abduction. UFO researcher Budd Hopkins has disclosed several "red flags" that abduction researchers look for in order to spot a possible missing-time abduction.

One clue is seeing an object in one location, and then instantly seeing the object in another location. This sudden "jump of locations" is often attributable to missing-time abduction. Another element is when the witnesses display an unreasonable fear after the encounter. Under hypnosis, many UFO witnesses discover that their encounters were much closer than they had first remembered.

UFO investigator Donald Webb has stated that perhaps as many as one in ten sightings could also be an abduction. Budd Hopkins has uncovered several cases in which the witnesses were not even aware of the missing time, but assumed that they only had a sighting.

After going over Grant's story, I realized that all the elements of a missing-time abduction were there. Grant felt they were being watched. The objects swooped towards them, and then there was a strange shift, and the objects were suddenly moving away, leaving both witnesses in a state of shock and fear. It fit the perfect pattern of a missing-time abduction.

Another early sighting occurred near Entrada on a summer night in 1986 when three witnesses saw two anomalous star-like objects. One of the witnesses, Vadja Potenza said, "These two star-like things came together and rotated around each other, and then separated . . . I didn't think it was a plane because I'd never seen any planes that could do that."

Vadja's friend, Gabe Aldort recalled, "They looked like stars and they came together and they stopped. They circled around each other. Then they both took off really fast. It was really weird and I knew planes couldn't do that."

This sighting, although simple, deeply impressed the witnesses. However, months later, in February 1987, another incredible encounter gave a hint of the coming wave. In this case, four teenage boys, including Gabe Aldort, saw no less than five objects, one of which was very large and emitted a beam of light next to the frightened witnesses.

All four were sitting on the porch of a home along Old Canyon when they saw a "weird-looking sports car-shaped [object]" fly overhead, followed by two identical-looking objects.

This was followed by the large object. "This thing was big," Gabe reported. "It wasn't a saucer or anything . . . it was square-shaped. It didn't have any lights on the bottom. All we saw was a shadow. And it came right over his house. And this beam came down and it moved across this particular part of the house . . . the beam came down and then it sucked back up again."

All four heard only a low buzzing hum. Gabe also noticed that the large object seemed to become transparent as it left. "It didn't go off into the distance. It's just like it faded. It just disappeared if that makes any sense."

Gabe's friend, John Heldman, described the large object as having "little lights on the outside of it, all the way around. And then it shined a beam down onto the house . . . it was a like a spotlight. In radius, it covered the whole house . . . we hid [beside] the house . . . I was kind of scared." The third witness, Ivan Eason recalled, "This big one . . . it shined this light on us . . . it just kind of went from one edge of the house to the other edge of the house where we were standing." After the large object left, a fifth smaller object followed that was identical to the first three, leaving all four witnesses in varying states of fear and disbelief. Gabe spoke eloquently for them all when he said, "I was so shocked . . . it just took our breath away. We couldn't believe it."

After investigating these encounters, I sent reports off to the *Messenger*. The editor, Colin Penno, printed the article in the January 1989 issue. I was disappointed when there was very little reaction to the story. I had hoped that article would prompt more people to reveal their own accounts. I couldn't understand why only my friends were seeing UFOs over Topanga. It didn't make any sense. Where were the other witnesses?

I chalked up these encounters to coincidence and concentrated my energy on the many other cases that were coming my way. It wasn't until over three years later that an incident of extraordinary complexity would grip the entire community and open the floodgates for scores of UFO eyewitnesses who had just been waiting for the right time to tell their stories.

2

June 14, 1992: The Wave Begins

In late June 1992, I received a call from my editor Colin Penno. He told me about a series of dramatic UFO incidents that had occurred over Topanga Canyon a week earlier. He'd planned to write a feature article about the incident. He called me because I had written the article that first generated his own interest in the subject. He thought I would also be interested.

I was, of course, more than interested. I was stunned. I simply couldn't grasp the magnitude of what was happening. I had been studying UFOs for over six years when suddenly, a UFO wave of enormous proportions was occurring right in my own backyard.

I couldn't wait for the article to come out. Colin evidently couldn't either, for it appeared on the cover of the next issue. The July cover story of the *Messenger* read "UFOs Over Topanga: The Sixth Encounter—They Came Once More." It is reproduced here in its entirety:

Sometime between midnight and dawn's early light Sunday, June 14, strange things happened in the night sky over Topanga.

We can't account for it, we can't explain it—and those who could just aren't talking.

Here's what we think we know . . .

From somewhere in West Hollywood, a couple of weeks ago a shaken man called the Lost Hills/Malibu sheriff's station to ask a question and tell a tale.

They'd eaten dinner down on the beach at Gladstones, and then he and his girlfriend took off for a spin up the Coast, turning north into the Santa Monica Mountains on Highway 27 for a peaceful night drive through Topanga Canyon and home to the bright lights of LA.

"Did anyone report anything strange tonight in Topanga Canyon?" came the call.

"Wanna be more specific?" responded a dubious deputy. "Strange like what?"

"Ah . . . lights."

"Not that I know of."

With his question answered, the caller stumbled into an incredible story.

"You'll think I'm crazy, but I don't know who to tell," he began.

"Officer, we were driving through the Canyon, where the Canyon gets deep, and we noticed a bright light in the sky." The couple became uneasy because they felt it was following them—whatever it was.

"Suddenly, it was over us, we lost control of the car and it lifted us up in the sky, lifted us up off the ground.

"I'm telling you, I've never been more frightened in my life," he said, assuring the cop that "we don't drink, don't take drugs and have no history of psychological problems."

What happened next was vague, according to the driver, who reckons they both lost memory for "I don't know, maybe a couple of minutes and then we were put down.

"Suddenly it (the light, the craft, the tractor beam) wasn't there any more."

Responding to a distraught but cogent caller, the listening officer stepped in from the cold of incredulity and asked were they both okay?

"Well we got home by the grace of God. My girlfriend was near-hysterical, we feel nauseated and weak, I don't know what to do.

"I'm telling you I'm a normal human being," the caller pleaded in a quaking voice.

"I have a job, a good job, and my girlfriend too. Should I report this . . . ? They'll think we're out of our minds!"

"I don't believe that something like this would fall under our jurisdiction," the cop said—and wrapped it up by advising the couple to sleep on it and maybe check in with a doctor in the morning.

SECOND FISHY COUPLE

Soon a second call about the state of cosmic stability in Topanga came in to the station.

"My girlfriend and I saw three very strange . . . ah, God . . . who does one report UFOs to?

"We saw three UFOs, flying discs high up in the Canyon, past the Sassafras Nursery, where the canyon gets deep."

"What did they look like?" inquired the voice of the law . . .

"They were saucers, they were following us above the car and we stopped to get out. We saw them, we watched them and within maybe three seconds—poof—they were gone straight up into the air like a bat out of hell."

This second caller was quite calm, we're told, and asked the listening deputy if he happened to have a number for the U.S. Air Force?

Disappointed, the second caller said, "Well, I dunno . . . we saw what we saw, maybe Gladstones spiked our wine?"

THE ODD NEW ENGLISHMAN

Next comes a call from a guy asking if the cops had helicopters flying over the Canyon that night—choppers with unusually bright lights?

"My wife and I were woken up by a very bright light above our home coming in through the windows," he says. "We went outside to look at . . . an extremely bright light . . . but there was hardly any sound," just a sort of "high-pitched hum."

His home and the "encounter" were about a mile north of Sassafras, they answered in response to a deputy's question, but declined to give an address explaining that he really didn't want to report a UFO because his wife was "a bit shaken up right now."

"Have you eaten at Gladstones recently?" asked the deputy—still pushing for a location and explaining that maybe something illegal is going on.

"Deputy," the caller replied, "let me tell you this—if someone is doing something illegal around here they have a hell of a lot of wattage.

"Damnedest thing I ever saw in my life," he concluded, and hung up.

LAST CALL FROM TEXAS

Lastly that night came a call from a guy with a soft Texas accent—a guy who gave his name right up front.

"Did y'all have helicopters up in Topanga Canyon tonight?"

"What did you see?" inquired a deputy long-since accustomed to curious calls from a quixotic Canyon.

"I was going down through Topanga Canyon and I think they were helicopters 'cause they were shining damn bright lights on me, but they kind of chased me down the road a bit.

"It sure did put out a powerful beam, a very bright light," the cowboy went on. "I'd say they tailgated me from above, but I couldn't see anything 'cause it was so damned bright . . . it sure seemed strange to me."

WHAT THE DOCTOR SAW

For readers skeptical about outrageous stories from odd outsiders, here is testimony from a true Topangan with the guts to stand up and say what he saw!

Dr. Murray Clarke lives on Callon, a T-junction street at the termination of Cheney Drive, itself an eastward artery off Topanga Canyon Boulevard.

Clarke was up and about after midnight that Sunday morning June 14, when a powerful point of light zoomed over his house, heading north.

"I looked through my view window which faces the ridgeline and the Valley," Clarke told the *Messenger* last week. "It was traveling south-to-north very fast in a horizontal path, an intense yellow-white light. As it sped away from me—about over the last ridge, it just vanished."

Clarke, a homeopathic specialist in private practice in Santa Monica, estimated the entire incident to have lasted "just two or three seconds."

He went outside, naturally, but the night sky was "as it was before."

A burning meteor perhaps? A helicopter searchlight?

No says Clarke: "meteorites do not travel on a path parallel with the planet, and the intensity of the light was something no helicopter could have brought about."

THE HILLSIDE OBSERVATION

Around that time and a mile or so south of Clarke's house another Topanga resident remembers something she'd never seen before that night.

She too lives east of the Boulevard, and at an elevation similar to Clarke's—two or three hundred feet up from the canyon floor.

"I saw a brilliant ray of light outside through my window," says the witness, who prefers to be unidentified.

"I saw it and I'll never forget it," she told the *Messenger* last week. "I'm telling you this now, but, well, I'm a professional person and I can't afford the risk of ridicule."

The beam of a car on its way home in the neighborhood?

No way, she says.

"I've lived right here for years and because of the hills around I can tell you no headlights can pass around by the house."

A sheriff's chopper looking for who-knows-what in the night?

"I've seen those lights over and over," she shot back. "This light was so focused, so intense—like nothing I'd ever seen."

SO WHAT'S NEW?

None of this comes as much surprise to Preston Dennett, who wrote, "UFOs Over Topanga," a *Messenger* cover story in Volume 12, No. 25, our terminal edition of 1988.

Dennett says of last month's strange events: "This would be at least the sixth encounter in the Canyon."

The article's publication sent immediate shock waves through the community. Calls and letters poured in to the office of the *Messenger*. Some called to congratulate Colin and commend him for his bravery in publishing it. Others berated him for printing such "obvious trash." Many called to report their own sightings.

The article also generated interest outside of Topanga. Local UFO groups called. Strangers walked into the office requesting copies. It was eventually picked up the *UFO Newsclipping Service*, which distributed the story worldwide.

Popular newspapers picked up the story. On July 9, 1992, the *Los Angeles Times* printed a tongue-in-cheek article by Steve Harvey, in his column "Only In LA." The editorial first displayed the headline of Penno's article and commented, "Stop the presses: front-page headline in the Topanga *Messenger* Newspaper." Harvey then wrote a severely edited version of the article, saying nothing more than that a UFO was seen over Topanga. Then he wrote, "This brings up an interesting philosophical point, namely, What constitutes a UFO in Topanga?"

Despite the underlying ridicule, Harvey actually helped to bolster the controversy. He wrote, "Sheriff's Deputy Michael Gurrola confirmed that such a call was received from an individual who talked of a bright light coming over the car and lifting it up. He said the vehicle was transported a certain distance. There was no damage to the car, and no harm to them."

Harvey closed with the comment, "The *Messenger* adds that at least five other UFO contacts have been reported in Topanga in recent years. But it couldn't be established how many of these encounters also followed a night of dining at Gladstones."

Actually, such a fact could have been established quite easily. I was, of course, disappointed that Penno's article wasn't treated more seriously.

Other accounts were not much better. The Daily News briefly mentioned the encounter in "Country Living," by *Times* staff writer Scott Harris, in the Sunday, October 11, 1992 issue. The article focused on various aspects of Topanga, including the UFO encounters. Harris wrote, "Only a few [residents] say they saw a UFO swoop down through their canyon in the pre-dawn hours of Sunday, June 14, 1992. (It was by some accounts, Topanga's sixth such visitation.)"

The article eventually found its way into a popular UFO book published in England. *Alien Update,* by famed UFO researcher Timothy Good, presents the best reports from across the world dating from July 1991 to August 1992. Over one hundred accounts are presented, with the Topanga case being only one.

Topanga residents reacted differently to the news. Several letters were sent to the *Messenger* concerning the article, three of which were printed.

One letter, from Stephen Maples, is titled "Mother Ships From Alpha Beta Centauri." It is reproduced here in its entirety:

> So, UFOs over Topanga, eh?
>
> Flying discs, bright lights, cars in tractor beams, hot time in the old town tonight.
>
> I'm up well past midnight during most of the summer, but the strangest thing I've ever run into is my neighbor Scott Ratner leaving for work at 4:00 A.M. Strange? Undoubtedly. Terrifying? Usually. A creature from another planet? Well . . .
>
> Ironically, the same day I read the *Messenger* article regarding otherworldly visits, the *Los Angeles Times* included in its "Things To Do Over The Weekend" section a blurb regarding Abductees Day. It seems that the Third Annual UFO Abductees/Contactees Get Together was held Sunday at the Descanso Gardens in Flintridge.
>
> Why those gardens? Why in Flintridge? I have a friend who is from Flintridge. Doctor Brock may be an indication of why that particular site was chosen. Does he meet the criteria?

17

Strange? Undoubtedly. Terrifying? Usually. A creature from another planet? Well . . .

I have a large number of clients, as well as quite a few employees, who I have always maintained are living proof of beings from another planet inhabiting Earth.

Frankly the notion that life forms with the intelligence, capabilities, and inclination to travel vast distances of space wasting time buzzing cars in Topanga strikes me as a bit odd.

Perhaps these are Adolescent Life Forms from Elsewhere, and this is how they get their laughs. I participated in a few teenage rituals that were far more disruptive to lower life forms than the late night encounters described in the *Messenger* article.

Of course, the notion that these other beings are slipping through the cracks of our civil defense network and plucking hapless early hour travelers for study or odd sexual rituals is possible. On the other hand, I tend to think that if that was the purpose their methods would be a tad more overbearing.

I mean, if they can put together the technology to scramble across a few billion light years of space, in ships with the lighting capacity of a major U.S. city, and disappear in the blink of an eye, why don't they just settle down over a stretch of the Santa Monica Freeway on a typical Monday morning and take a good cross section of the local populace?

At the very least the mundaneness of Bill Keene's traffic reports would get a bit broken up.

18

"The 405 is crawling around an over-turned big rig, the brushfire next to the Pomona Freeway has things slow out there, but the good news is that the Santa Monica Freeway coming into town is clear sailing. Another one of those mother ships from Alpha Beta Centaur has swept up all the cars from La Cienega to La Brea eastbound."

There is no hard or fast rules in my game of life. As a non-practicing atheist and a devoted agnostic, should I die and discover that there really is a God, I'm prepared to say "oops." So, if this clandestine approach to the human race turns out to be the course chose by our visitors from other worlds, I can accept it. However, their stock with me will drop just a hair or two.

I see a bit more in the article than meets the eye. Our dear editor, Colin Penno, refers in his article to the Odd New Englishman. Those of us who have had the pleasure can certainly attest that the *Messenger's* illustrious leader is a bit odd, and he just may be vain enough to consider himself new, and he is without a doubt an Englishman.

So, maybe, just maybe, this whole article is one of those pathetic shrieks in the night for which journalists are so well known. The rigors, stress and strain of the rag trade may have caught up with the editor and this is his cry for help.

I would not, however, call Penno's article a "cry for help." In fact, Penno related to me that he was somewhat anxious about how people might react. Although Maples' letter does raise some interesting points, it falls short of seriously addressing the issue.

Of course the *Messenger* received more than one letter. One of the letters, however, stood out from all the rest. One of the strangest letters ever published in the *Messenger*, it is called "Ticket from the Stars," which was written by someone who goes by the name, XaLanKTon "BuzzY" GlepNOck. Here it is in its entirety:

I am sending this message to your newspaper in the hope that you will convey my apologies to the denizens of the Topanga Canyon area.

On June 14, 1992, my friends and I "borrowed" my parents' vehicle and went joyriding through the Canyon. After recklessly speeding about and scaring innocent bystanders, we journeyed home thinking "no harm, no foul." Little did I realize how much harm my friends and I caused. My parents reported their vehicle stolen and the authorities pulled us over just before we reached our home destination. The result: a judge ordered me to write an apology to Topangans.

In addition, my saucer privileges have been suspended for 23.8 quodras. Furthermore, my parents have taken away my transporter, bleem stick, and star-phase integrator.

I realize now that my actions were immature and reckless. Using our tractor beam not only endangered the lives of helpless Topangans, but it also could have seriously altered the current friendship between our races. (I am sending an apology to our two Earth-bound ambassadors, Dan Quayle and Jerry Brown, as well.) I will never do these types of things again.

> Please accept my apologies, and if you're ever
> on Alpha Beta Centauri, please drop by and say
> blix (remember, we don't take double coupons.)

Although the letter is admittedly very funny, I wonder how the couple who were picked up by the UFO would feel about it. More than likely, they would not be amused.

Another letter of a more serious nature was submitted by Topanga resident Woody Hastings. The letter was titled "The Sixth Encounter: Ball Lightning or Bolide," and published in the same issue as Maples' letter. This is Hastings' reaction to the article:

> The cover story on the event of Sunday June 14 is
> quite intriguing. Before I continue, I would like to
> make a clarification that may seem obvious, but I
> feel is important.
>
> The term UFO is too often and too easily used
> to refer to extraterrestrial alien spacecraft. UFO
> stands for unidentified flying object, and that is
> what the vast majority of sightings always
> remain—unidentified. It will surely be a great day
> when we finally make contact with an IFO (iden-
> tified flying object) and that IFO is indeed benev-
> olent visitors from deep space. With that out of
> the way, I would like to examine what happened
> on the 14th.
>
> In the case of the unidentified "odd outsider"
> (UOO?) who claims to have had his car lifted from
> the Earth, perhaps the only explanation is that
> intelligent creatures did indeed visit Topanga. The
> fact that they are intelligent is further bolstered by

the fact that they avoided the rest of Los Angeles and headed straight for Topanga.

In the case of the implicitly more reliable "testimony from a true Topangan" (TTT?) there happens to be a somewhat more conventional explanation that fits his description, as well as most of the others.

Dr. Clarke describes what he saw as a "powerful point of light [that] zoomed over [his] house heading north . . . an intense yellow-white light . . . traveling . . . very fast in a horizontal path." He goes on to say that "meteorites (sic) do not travel on a path parallel with the planet." (Meteorites are the actual space rocks that you find after a meteor, more commonly known as a shooting star, though not a star at all, has made it through the Earth's atmosphere and actually landed on Earth.)

Surprisingly, the fact is that some meteors do actually travel in a horizontal path through the Earth's atmosphere!

Meteors usually enter the Earth's atmosphere at an angle steep enough to allow the object to reach such a great speed that the heat from friction with the atmosphere causes the object to glow and then rapidly burn out in a flash as it plunges toward the planet. The great majority of these objects never make it to Earth in one piece, but remnants of meteors, in the form of space dust, do rain down all over the planet each day.

The phenomenon that may have been witnessed on June 14 occurs when an object in space enters the Earth's atmosphere at a very shallow angle. Like a stone skipping across the lake, the object either glances off the outer atmosphere, back out into space, or skims along a layer of the atmosphere at very high velocity, glowing from the heat of the friction. These types of meteors are generally called bolides and are very rare but also very real. Needless to say, bolides put on quite a light show by most accounts, and some have even been visible in broad daylight.

In 1972 "a most remarkable case of an object that almost became a meteorite occurred . . . when a body calculated to be about the size of a house entered the Earth's atmosphere. Its path carried it parallel to the Earth's surface about 60 kilometers above the ground over the Rocky Mountains. It left the atmosphere over southern Canada and continued in orbit around the Sun." (From an account in the book *Exploring the Universe* by Protheroe, Capriotti, Newsom.) This event was witnessed by many people, photographed and even captured on a tourist's 8mm movie camera. It certainly looked like it could have been an alien spacecraft, but alas, it was just a hot space rock.

If the object in question was a bolide, certainly it would have been visible to other people in the Los Angeles basin, but then again, if it was an alien spacecraft would that not also have been visible to others outside of Topanga? In a follow up, I would like to know if there were concurrent sightings that night outside of Topanga.

One other possibility that would explain why the event was observed only in Topanga is that what occurred was the even more rare and exotic phenomenon known as ball lightning. Ball lightning would have fit the bill for the Sunday sightings but is usually associated with electrical storm activity. I happened to be in Brazil on the 14th; were there storms?

Perhaps the object over Topanga on June 14 will never become an IFO but I really don't think it helps anything to jump to the conclusion that we (Topangans) are being regularly visited by alien space creatures. Though I believe we can be fairly sure that the universe is absolutely teeming with life, intelligent creatures that have developed a stable technological civilization are however, probably quite rare, and a visit by them would be even more rare.

But is Woody Hastings correct? Could the sightings be explained as meteors, bolides, or ball lightning? Unfortunately, Hastings has made the common error of ignoring the data to fit his theory.

A simple examination of the testimonies shows that it could not have been a meteor, bolide or ball lightning. The evening was perfectly clear; there was no storm activity. Over nine adults were sufficiently impressed by what they saw to call either the police or the newspaper.

Dr. Clarke's observation is not consistent with a shooting star or a bolide. Both of these leave bright blazing paths in the atmosphere. Dr. Clarke saw only a point of light. And taken alone, his observation was not that impressive.

But at the same time, another woman called the newspaper to report that she saw an extremely bright "ray of light" outside her window. This again, does not match a shooting star, but it does match the report from the man who called to say that something chased him down the boulevard, tailgating him from above, shining down powerful beams of light.

Then there's the call from the Englishman and his wife who were awakened by a "very bright light above our home." Going outside to investigate, they saw the light hovering and heard a strange high-pitched hum.

And what about the call from the people who ate at Gladstones and decided to drive through Topanga Canyon? Their stories are also very similar. One man called to say that he and his girlfriend were chased by "three UFOs, flying disks, high up in the canyon." This hardly sounds like a shooting star.

The clincher, however, comes from the first couple who called to say that their car was actually lifted up by the light as it chased them up the road. I could tell that the couple was obviously badly shaken. As the caller said, "We got home by the grace of God. My girlfriend was nearly hysterical, we feel [nauseated] and weak, I don't know what to do." I have yet to meet anybody whose car was lifted up off the road by a shooting star.

Remember none of these people had any idea that there had been other callers. They are only reporting what happened to them. It is as if each of them saw only snippets of what actually happened. Some saw merely unexplained lights. Some saw actual disk-shaped craft. And at least one couple appears to have experienced a missing-time abduction.

As any UFO investigator will tell you, the great majority of UFO sightings go unreported. In this case, over six reports were made on a single evening. Because of this, I knew that possibly dozens of other people also saw UFOs on June 14, but didn't know what they were seeing, much less who to call. I was not mistaken.

After the *Messenger* article came out, the office of the newspaper began receiving calls from other witnesses. Now that the first witnesses had bravely stepped forward and told their stories, other people were ready to tell what they saw. Colin graciously referred the callers to me.

And so began my investigation to find out what really happened on June 14, 1992.

3

June 14, 1992: Confirmation

THE FIRST STEP in my investigation: call the Malibu Police. I explained to them I was investigating UFO sightings in the Topanga Canyon area. They verified that on June 14 they did receive four separate calls regarding UFOs. The conversations were, of course, recorded. When I asked if they could release the tape conversations, the officer on duty answered, "Not without a court order." Because the callers were anonymous, I was never able to interview them.

On a subsequent call to the police, another officer told me that they receive UFO reports regularly, at least a few every year. The officer agreed to take down my name and number and refer any callers to me. It wouldn't be long before I started to get those calls.

My next step was to question the Topanga State Park Rangers who patrol the park. None of them reported seeing anything unusual or receiving any reports of UFOs. I called a physician who practices in

Topanga and asked him if he had any patients who reported UFOs. One of his patients mentioned something about UFOs, but he couldn't recall any details. I asked the manager and employees of the local metaphysical bookstore if they had received any reports. Although they expressed an interest in the subject, to their knowledge nobody had come to the bookstore to ask about UFOs.

Although I followed all the official avenues of investigation, I was unable to find any additional corroboration that UFOs had visited Topanga on June 14.

My next step was to call every Topanga resident I knew and slip in that crucial question, "Where were you on June 14? Did you see anything unusual?" I called over a dozen people, but none of them saw anything unusual. Almost all replied that they never even went outside that evening.

That evening, however, was not a normal evening. It also happened to be the night of a lunar eclipse. This alone should have caused many people to at least look outside.

I was in Topanga that evening and drove through the canyon around 9:00 P.M. Later on I went outside to look at the eclipse, but it was only for a few moments. Of course, I didn't see anything unusual. I know of two other people who were also in Topanga that evening and went outside to look at the eclipse. Neither of them saw anything unusual.

Just when I was despairing of finding any additional witnesses, all my calling finally paid off. When I called each person, I asked them to ask their friends about anything unusual they had seen on June 14. Within two

28

weeks of making the initial calls, two people called me back. Both reported that they had found additional witnesses. Both said that the witnesses were willing to speak with me. Interviews with the witnesses were quickly set up. I was, of course, very eager to hear what they had to say.

The first confirmation that unidentified flying objects visited Topanga came from Phillip and Mandy, who live in the San Fernando Valley. Phillip and Mandy also have friends who live in Topanga Canyon.

Their friends in Topanga invited Phillip and Mandy to dinner and to watch the lunar eclipse with them on the evening of June 14. Phillip and Mandy drove up early in the evening to their friends' home on Entrada, ate dinner, and spent the evening talking and watching the Earth's shadow gradually cover the surface of the moon.

Phillip, however, had to work the next morning, so they said their goodbyes and left. Just after midnight, they turned off Entrada and headed north up Topanga Canyon Boulevard. Despite the lateness of the hour, Phillip remembered seeing a few other cars traveling along the boulevard. It was a warm evening and they had the windows down to enjoy the breeze.

Almost immediately after they turned onto the boulevard, Mandy noticed what she at first thought were helicopters. As she watched, however, she realized there was something strange about them. They not only didn't look like helicopters, but they moved very quickly and seemed to dart around. And, even stranger, they were totally silent. As Mandy said, "That was about midnight. We were coming home. And just a few minutes after we pulled onto Topanga Canyon, all of a sudden, there were several of them. I can't remember the numbers now, but it was like five. Five or six huge bright lights moving at all different angles."

Mandy admitted she wasn't paying close attention to the objects, but they were so strange that she kept wondering what could be happening. As they drove down the boulevard, she kept glancing at the strange glowing objects, trying to figure out what they were. At times, she said, the objects actually followed their vehicle. "We were followed—definitely followed—half way down the mountain, the whole drive down, until we got to the very bottom. I thought they were helicopters except they were totally silent. These brilliant lights were just all over us as we were driving down the mountain. And I thought there was a drug bust or something like that. The lights were incredibly bright. Pure white lights. But they made absolutely no sound. I was just convinced they were helicopters, but we had the windows rolled down and they weren't making any noise. It was completely unexplained. We had no idea what they could have been. But they followed us all the way down, all the way down the mountain."

Phillip didn't pay any attention to what was happening until they had reached the straightaway that leads out of Topanga and down into the San Fernando Valley. At the moment that they were about to leave Topanga, something caught Phillip's eye. To his surprise, he got a clear view of three brightly lit saucer-shaped objects in a triangular formation, floating over Henry Ridge into Topanga Canyon. Phillip turned to his wife and said, "Look! . . . flying saucers!"

At first he was only joking. After all, the last thing you expect to see are UFOs. It wasn't until he looked again that he realized it was no joke. The objects really did look like flying saucers.

As Phillip recalled, "I saw three craft coming over the hill. There appeared to be some lights on them. And I jokingly turned to Mandy and said, 'Oh, look, Mandy! There are flying saucers!' And she thought I was kidding. You know, I wasn't really sure, but it did look like it, and they appeared to be silently floating, just moving over the hills. And it appeared to me they were pretty close to the ground. It wasn't like they were way up in the sky."

Even though the objects looked and moved strangely, Phillip found himself unable to believe that he was actually observing UFOs. As he said, "I thought they might have been helicopters. When I looked at them, they appeared to be close enough. Now they could have been much higher and larger than I thought they were, but the only explanation my mind could give me was that they were helicopters. I was driving, so I looked at them. I got a flash that they could have been flying saucers, but then I had to put my eyes back on the road, so I didn't pull over and spend a whole lot of time watching them . . . my first impression was that they were flying saucers, in that they appeared to be easily floating and moving over the hills, reminiscent somewhat of what we see in the movies."

What most impressed Phillip was the strange appearance of the objects. These were not amorphous, unexplained lights. As he says, "They were definable. They were craft. As a matter of fact, there seemed to be lighting on the craft, which is why, after I made my joke and I wasn't really sure, I just discarded it because I didn't expect to see a flying saucer that close in such a highly inhabited area. It just didn't make any sense. So I said, 'Oh, it must be some kind of craft.'

"But it did appear to have some kind of lighting on it . . . it seemed to have separate lights if I recall correctly. And this is very weak recall at this point; there may have been a whitish, orangish and red light, but I'm not certain about that. There appeared to be a dark body behind the lights. It wasn't just like a little spot of light in the sky . . . it was odd. It was clearly odd. It was not a craft I could identify readily. I couldn't."

One of the telltale marks of an unidentified flying object is its strange appearance. Another element that investigators look for is unusual movement. This detail figures prominently in Phillip's report. "They came over the hill and they sort of followed the contour of the land . . . you know how with automobiles, you can get a governor for speed? It was almost as if they had a height-governor, as if they knew exactly how high they wanted to be, and just sort of followed the contour."

At the time, Phillip and Mandy couldn't believe they were actually seeing UFOs. The two of them just kept driving out of the canyon and into the valley. It wasn't until a few weeks later that their friends from Topanga called and asked if they saw anything strange that night.

Phillip replied that they had seen something strange and briefly described what they saw. Only then were they told about what other witnesses had seen that night.

Phillip and Mandy now believe that whatever occurred on that night, they witnessed only a small glimpse. Unknown to either of them at the time, many other people in Topanga were experiencing much more dramatic encounters that night. Phillip and Mandy reached home around 12:30 A.M. At that exact time, the objects were chasing other cars down the boulevard, shining dazzling beams of light into people's homes and putting on a display that would send shock waves through Topanga.

With the addition of Phillip's and Mandy's reports, the picture became clearer about the evening in question. Still there were many missing pieces to the story. If so many people saw the objects, how many were there? Where were they coming from? Where were they going? How long did the activity last?

The answer to all these questions was provided by a wonderful couple who just happened to be in a position to observe virtually the entire UFO incident. This couple, Daniel and Katherine, has lived in Topanga for many years. Their house is perched high on the ridge of Saddlepeak, one of the highest points in Topanga, with a panoramic view of the Pacific ocean, Santa Monica, Malibu, the San Fernando Valley, and of course, Topanga Canyon.

Before June 14, Daniel and Katherine had never seen anything unusual over Topanga. Daniel spent many years in the U. S. military and was quite familiar with aircraft. Many years ago, in Costa Mesa, California, he had seen an unidentified flying object. The object was witnessed by many other people, though was officially pronounced in the newspapers to be "unusual weather phenomenon." Other than that, neither of them had seen anything unusual flying in the skies.

Because they live high on the ridge, they often sit outside on their wood deck and watch the stars and the distant lights of the city. They are very familiar with the flight paths of the jets that pass over the nearby coast and land at Los Angeles International Airport.

June 14 changed all that. The first strange incident occurred early that morning. While in bed, Daniel and Katherine heard a humming noise coming from outside the house. Katherine turned to Daniel and asked him if he heard the noise. He said that he did, and they both went outside to search for the source.

They were unable to locate the sound, and eventually it stopped. Katherine remembered she jokingly told Daniel, "Maybe it's a spaceship."

Little did she know how prophetic those words would be.

Around sunset, Daniel and Katherine decided to sit down and watch a video. As the tape was rewinding, Katherine noticed pink flashes of light from outside towards the east. Although the sky was clear, she thought at first that the flashes were lightning. "I saw a flash of light, like pinkish lightning over there. I thought, 'Oh, that's strange pink lightning.' But I didn't think anything about it. But I kept seeing light out there. While Daniel was in the kitchen, we were waiting for the video to wind up, and I said, 'There's strange light out there, Daniel.' But it was no big deal. We just sort of went back to watching the video."

No sooner had they returned to the video when Katherine's attention was drawn to a large bar of light hovering outside. She looked at it and saw that it was a perfectly horizontal glowing line of light that seemed to be coming from behind the mountain to the southeast, over the southern area of Topanga Canyon. Katherine said, "It looked like a perfectly straight line of light, came out horizontally, which I thought was very strange. I said, 'Well, that's not lightning, you know. But I sort of dismissed it. I just thought, 'Oh, that's very weird.'"

By now, it was 8:30 P.M. and the sky was dark. Outside, their dogs began barking furiously and both Katherine and Daniel saw bright flashes of light coming from the same direction as before. Katherine recalled, "Suddenly, there were a lot of flashes of light from the same area, and then I became excited. I said, 'Daniel, look! There's a light!' And then he saw the light."

They went outside and looked towards the flashes. The bar of light Katherine had seen was gone, but just below where it had been, they both saw a large, oval-shaped, glowing object hovering just above the ridge.

Katherine described the object as "a white oval shape, like a white glow, just sitting there."

At first the object remained motionless. Then after about five or ten seconds, it suddenly disappeared and appeared instantaneously in another location slightly forward and to the right. In the original location another oval-shaped object appeared. As Daniel remembered, "Suddenly it went 'poof!' It disappeared and it appeared again. It was here and then it disappeared, went 'poof!' It was there instantaneously. And then it sat there for a while. And then another one appeared right where that one had disappeared."

The couple could now clearly see two objects hovering in the sky. Almost instantly, however, the first object began to move, and this time, it took off and headed straight towards them. Katherine said, "It was

35

as if this one moved up there to where the horizontal bar was that I had seen earlier, and another oval glow came to this location. Then the one that had moved up there would suddenly flash straight over our heads, lighting up the whole sky in almost a triangle shape."

Daniel and Katherine watched with surprise and awe as the second object moved upward and a third object appeared. Moments later, the second object flashed over their heads, the third object moved upward, and a fourth one appeared. As the second, third and fourth objects zipped overhead lighting up their entire house, and more objects continued to appear, Daniel and Katherine realized that something very unusual was happening. It was probably around this time that the police began receiving calls.

Said Daniel, "It sat there for a while, then it [went] 'shew!' . . . There was a number of them. This went on for quite a while, in a kind of rhythmic way. They would go directly overhead, right overhead, directly that way [northwest], in the same lines."

The couple couldn't tell for certain whether the objects were solid or just lights. They were very defined and definitely opaque, but they were also very bright and moved very fast. For these reasons, close observation was difficult. As Katherine recalled, "That's what we were trying to figure out. We were staring at them . . . trying to figure out, what is that exactly? . . . when it moved, it was just an intense light."

Said Daniel, "It was as if when you looked up at them, there was a bright light that was much brighter than the glow that was around them. The glow had a definite shape. It was an oval . . . we kept trying to see what shape that they were because they seemed just like a light moving, except that there were . . . like . . . coils. And what that was, the way it registered on the eye, really trying to concentrate, to me it was—Katherine said it too—it was a sine wave. You know what a sine wave is? In the center of the light was this very bright coil, sort of a sine wave shape."

One detail that impressed both of them was how the objects would suddenly stop and change their direction in mid-flight. As Daniel remembered, "Twice, one started out, it would stop, change at a ninety-degree angle: 'zoom-zoom-shew!' And it would move fast. . . . They would accelerate really fast. I don't know if that's because they were going in this direction, but it was fast. And every now and then, just a few times though, they'd start off in one direction, and then suddenly go make a right angle turn and go in the other way . . . every time one would change its mind, it would go 'shew!' I mean, start very quickly, at right angles . . . But most of the time they followed exactly."

After about fifteen minutes, the objects disappeared completely. Daniel and Katherine estimated that they had seen at least twenty objects. They were baffled that the objects emitted no noise whatsoever, but both of them were reluctant to say the word UFO. And since the night sky had suddenly returned to normal, they went back inside. Katherine admitted to being mildly alarmed at the sight of so many unexplained objects, but now that the encounter was over, they felt they could relax.

They turned the video back on and tried to resume watching it. After about fifteen minutes, another series of bright flashes drew their attention away from the video. They ran outside and to their surprise, the display was starting all over again. Quickly, one after another, more than ten objects appeared and zipped overhead. In a matter of minutes, the objects were gone. As Katherine said, "Sometimes one would wait there, like it would start to leave and then it would wait there . . . and you'd think, 'Well, what's it waiting for?' And then it would go 'shoot!' And then the other one, 'shoot!' And then 'shoot!' And then the other one would wait."

Daniel and Katherine returned inside wondering what to do. They decided to try again to watch their video. Within fifteen minutes, however, the flashes started up again. Again, they dashed out onto their deck and clung to each other as the objects appeared, darted around and whizzed in different directions. After four or five times, it looked like the objects would never stop coming. The sight of so many of them began to unnerve them. Katherine especially became upset and not a little frightened. The objects just kept coming!

As Katherine recalled, "Sometimes twenty of them would come. Sometimes we'd see four or five. . . . We'd be waiting. And then we'd say, 'Oh, it's over.' Then those flashes of light would come and we'd run back out on the porch and watch it. And I tried to sort of count it . . . sometimes it would be a five minute interval. Sometimes it would be fifteen minutes. A couple of times it was maybe twenty minutes to a half- hour."

Daniel also remembers how the objects came in groups, or as he says, "clusters, four or five, sometimes ten, a little more, twenty I guess, in clusters. Then it would stop. Then they'd suddenly go 'whoosh-whoosh-whoosh-whoosh!'"

By the fourth or fifth time the couple had stepped outside on the deck, Katherine was thoroughly upset. She counted the objects as they rose from behind the nearby ridge. And the numbers she came up with were, if you'll forgive the pun, astronomical.

But it was precisely because there were so many objects that Katherine began to keep count. "It would have to be a very bright light to get our attention because we weren't sitting right in front of the window. We were sitting in front of the television. But the lights were so bright, they would call our attention away from the television to the porch. And there were so many of them that I said, 'Well, let's count them.' And then after ten, then twelve, then fifteen, it was so many! And I said, 'Okay, that was about forty.'"

But that was only when the objects first began appearing. After over an hour of the activity, the number of them had climbed considerably. As Katherine recalled, "There were so many of them. We were so caught up in the excitement of it. We were so amazed. We kept thinking it would end. I was trying to keep count, though I'm sure it wasn't an exact count. It was like, 'Okay, that was about forty. Okay, that was about forty.' And I said that at least five times. So my estimation of how many lights, or how many flashes of these oval things we saw, was about two hundred. Now that was very frightening to me . . . that was very frightening to me that there were so many . . ."

Daniel didn't count the objects, but admits that Katherine was probably right. He could also tell how upset she was. As he recalled, "She was really frightened by how many. She said, 'Where are they all coming from? Where are they going?' It was frightening to her."

Katherine is sure there were at least two hundred objects. But as she said, "Daniel doesn't like me to say that there were two hundred of them, because he says that's too wild. Well that's exactly why it was so upsetting to me. I don't know if it makes it any more wild seeing a hundred as opposed to two hundred, but it was a lot."

It was also upsetting because they had no idea what the objects were. As Katherine said, "We've never seen anything like this. You can sit out here and watch the planes over LAX from here all night long, and I personally have never seen anything weird like that before in my entire life. Daniel said he's never seen it before. Daniel's been in the military and everything."

They both even wondered if perhaps they were seeing a military exercise of some sort. Katherine related, "We imagined that it was some sort of Air Force thing we were not informed of, that they were doing something with their military information that normal people don't get to hear about. But two hundred is still kind of a lot for that too, and it was very upsetting to me either way . . . it was so overwhelming . . . I said by the evening's end that those were either aliens or our own military movement. And in either case, I found it extremely upsetting and frightening. If our Air Force or whatever you want to call it is doing something to that degree without our knowledge, [then] what are they doing? And if it's extraterrestrials, what the hell are they doing here in so many ships? And why are they splitting now? Those questions were undeniable for me, and they were upsetting in either case."

Daniel felt certain, however, that the objects were not government or military test vehicles. "Whatever that is, or whatever they do, the point of it is, it doesn't behave like things are in nature, whatever their physics are. Just the acceleration . . . My feeling is that it's very possible they are extraterrestrials. I don't know that they're all in one group."

After watching the objects for hours, Daniel and Katherine began to notice predictable patterns. As Katherine said, "You know when you watch something for a while, you get a feeling? You watch ants going in a certain direction, you can figure out where they're coming from, the lines and so forth? So after watching them, you got the feeling that they were going all over this area from that certain spot right there . . . it just seemed like it was a mass evacuation to me, because I witnessed it. That's how I experienced it."

For anyone who thinks seeing UFOs is fun, Katherine had this to say: "It was not good news. I didn't sleep that night and I was upset for weeks after that . . . I always thought that if I saw an alien spaceship, that would be very exciting, and I would be happy. And if there were aliens from another planet, that I would want to meet them or experience them. But I have to say that was not my actual reaction. Maybe if it had been three or four, I would have thought, "Oh, that's very fascinating.' But because there were so many, I was very intimidated."

Daniel felt the same way. "If one of those stopped, I would hate that. The feeling is, what can you do? They'll do whatever they're going to do."

When the objects finally stopped appearing, Katherine was a nervous wreck. As she says, "At 10:30, we were out there waiting, waiting, waiting. And it was pretty clear that it was all done . . . we sort of kept watching, doing things around the house. We were all excited. It was hard to go to bed. The adrenaline was sort of going . . . we finally went into the bedroom. The bedroom's really closed off, but by then, I didn't want to see it anymore."

Said Daniel, "Actually, we tried to forget about it. It was really strange. We went through everything it could be."

The next morning, they decided to do some investigating. They called the *Los Angeles Times,* which was not interested in their story. They then called the Malibu/Lost Hills Police. The police were oddly interested in hearing their story, and even asked for drawings, but refused to say if there were any other reports. As Katherine said, "They wouldn't tell us anything that they had heard from anybody else, but they wanted to hear our story exactly, and they wanted us to [do] drawings and stuff like that. I said, 'Have you gotten any reports?' And they said, 'Well, what did you see exactly?'"

Katherine then called the office of a popular UFO magazine, but the editors replied that, without photographs, their story wouldn't make a good article. They told the frightened witnesses, "Well, how can we write an article around that?"

Daniel and Katherine then began calling their neighbors. To their surprise, nobody else saw anything that night. This strange lack of corroborating witnesses is typical of many UFO encounters, but it only served to mystify the couple. As Daniel said, "That was so weird because we kept thinking, 'People had to see that!'"

Said Katherine, "We called around and didn't get support. We were not that well received . . . it was already distressing to me. It's like being a victim of . . . abuse. You go through the stress and then nobody believes you. And you have to prove what happened. Although nothing really happened to me, it was just stressful to experience seeing so many things. And then trying to explain it to someone is one thing, but trying to convince someone that I'm telling the truth, that's hard."

They were very relieved when Penno's article was published. Only then did Katherine realize how lucky they were to have seen what they saw. "We sort of forgot about it until we saw that article saying that other people had seen things. When I read that article, I thought that they were seeing a few of them coming in at a time. We had a great view of all these things. But the people having these other sightings, it sounded like they were seeing three or four."

Said Daniel, "The same night, all the sightings that we read about were down below, near Entrada. They were all down below."

After reading the article, Katherine was surprised by her reaction. "We read that in the newspaper, then it's sort of like I don't know if I felt better or not, but at least I knew somebody else saw something. I knew I was seeing something because Daniel saw it too, and we saw it for two hours."

Since that incident, neither Daniel nor Katherine has seen any more objects.

So closes the saga of June 14, 1992. At least thirteen adults witnessed inexplicable activity. Eight separate reports were made by people who had no knowledge that other people were seeing the same thing.

The events of that night are now fairly clear. Around sunset, a large number of UFOs appeared from southern Topanga Canyon. They traveled in various directions for over two hours, from approximately 8:00 P.M. until 10:30 P.M. One or two hours later, two vehicles left Gladstones restaurant and traveled north up Topanga Canyon Boulevard. One car was chased by three objects. Another car was chased by one object, and then lifted up off the road. A third car heading north from Entrada up the boulevard was followed by several objects darting about the canyon. Meanwhile, a fourth car was heading south down Topanga Canyon Boulevard, and it was also chased by an unidentified flying object.

Two other Topanga residents, separated by about a mile, both reported seeing unusual light activity outside their windows.

It cannot be denied that something very unusual occurred on that amazing evening. But were they really alien spaceships?

The answer to that question and others may lie with the other people who read about the UFOs in the *Messenger* and were inspired to call and tell their own stories. One after another, additional witnesses came forth. However, the witnesses were saying that they had seen unidentified objects over Topanga in the days and weeks following the June 14 incident.

One fact suddenly became clear. Whatever the objects were, they showed no signs of leaving. In fact, Topanga appeared to be in the middle of a UFO wave of gigantic proportions.

4

The Wave Continues

$\mathcal{J}$ANICE WAS THE first wit-
ness to call the *Messenger* in response to the article, and
she usually lives in Santa Barbara, California. However,
she had a friend in Topanga Canyon who needed a
housesitter during the summer of 1992. Janice eagerly
jumped at the chance. She and her boyfriend, John, had
discovered Topanga the year before and instantly fell in
love with it. Spending the summer in the peaceful
canyon sounded like a dream come true.

John, however, lived in the San Fernando Valley,
and they often commuted back and forth to each
other's homes. This, of course, involved many late
night drives through the dark canyon.

On one of these drives Janice had what was to be
the first of a series of encounters. Although she does-
n't remember the exact day, she knows it was either
the second or third week in June, 1992. At about
11:15 P.M. she headed south on the boulevard somewhere around the center of the canyon when she saw

45

a sudden, intense flash of brilliant light flood a portion of the night sky.

It happened so quickly that Janice barely had time to react. As she said, "There was a bright floodlight— seemingly a floodlight—in the sky, and it was on the left side of the road. And it just flashed and it was gone . . . there weren't rays like it was a beam of light. It was like a floodlight that would just come on and off."

Janice was startled by the strange flash of light, but didn't think much of it. The *Messenger* story hadn't yet been printed, so she was unaware of the strange occurrences in the canyon.

A few days later, Janice was again traveling into the canyon at around the same time. She was passing the same general location when again, the sky towards the east flared up in brilliant light. But as quickly as it flashed on, the light flashed off. As Janice says, "It was just a flash, just 'poof,' just a flash."

Because the flash was so brief, Janice kept driving. As she drove, she remembered seeing the strange light a few days earlier and wondered again what caused it. Nothing came to mind, so Janice just pushed the incident out of her mind and returned home.

About one week after the second incident, Janice was driving through the same area at the same time. This time, however, John was with her. Janice had never even mentioned the previous incidents. It just didn't seem important.

Then the light flashed again. This time, Janice couldn't deny that something strange was happening. As she recalled, "The first time, I just disregarded it. And the next time I saw it, I thought, 'Wait a minute.

What's that? I saw that before.' And the next time, it was with my boyfriend, and I realized that I was definitely seeing something."

John had no idea that Janice had seen strange flashes of light, so when it happened to him, he was taken by complete surprise. Nevertheless, he gave a very vivid description. "We were, of course, driving through the canyon. And we got to the deep part, where the canyon gets dark . . . anyway, I saw this light out of the corner of my left eye. And I remember that it was so intense, I could feel it physically. I could feel the light physically. Most light, you see the light and you kind of glance at it. This one I could feel. It almost like touched the center of your body.

"And I glanced immediately to my left up into the sky, and it had gone. And of course, we were very curious about it, so we turned around and drove back, and took the same path through and through. And we didn't see it again after that.

"But the light was an intensity I can only describe in very few words. I don't know what else to say to describe it. It was just so intense, you could feel it physically."

Although the flash was brief, John believes that he turned his head just in time to see the source of illumination. In fact, he remembers having a strong impulse to suddenly look in that direction. The impulse was so strong and out of character, that it seemed almost like telepathy. Because of this, he was able to get a good view. As he says, "The flash, it was in the shape of an egg, that's how I remember it, kind of an oval shape— a giant egg. It was about the size of a spotlight, only an egg shape. An egg-shaped spotlight. It was so brief that by the time it happened in the sky, I turned to look, it was already gone . . . I didn't hear anything, not that I remember. It was just the strangest thing. The light was very, very intense and it was a white light. It had like a bluish-purple aura around it."

Although a flash of light may sound innocuous, John was deeply impressed by its strangeness. He also noticed that the light was strangely localized. "Here's a good way to describe this light. It's extremely intense and extremely bright, and like I said, you can feel it physically; yet it does not light up the area around it at all . . . I think that's very strange, that there would be a light that's so intense, yet does not light up the area around it at all."

After searching for a while, John and Janice finally drove home. They continued to discuss the incident, but couldn't figure out what it was. Only then did John learn that Janice had already seen the light twice before.

By now, they had learned to keep their eyes open. Whenever they drove through the canyon, they kept a lookout for strange flashes of light.

To their surprise, less than a week after the third sighting, they were driving through the same area when the light flashed again. To their disappointment, the flash was so brief that they didn't get a good look. As John said, "I don't know. As soon as it flashes on, you try to look at it, and it just . . . it's gone! It's like looking at the sun almost, [except it's] nighttime, only it's localized, and the beam of light from it is very . . . narrow."

After that occasion, they never saw the light flash again. However, from the middle of June to the beginning of July, they had seen the strange light a total of four times.

Then on July 5, Janice glanced at a copy of the *Messenger* and saw the UFO story on the front cover. At that point, she realized that she and John had probably seen the UFOs. Janice called the *Messenger* and told them her story.

Although Janice and John feel that their sightings were unexplainable, both of them were eager to see something more substantial. Unfortunately, the summer and the housesitting job ended, and Janice moved back to Santa Barbara.

Although Janice and John didn't know it, their observations were greatly significant. The mysterious flashes of light they had seen were coming directly from an area where another family was experiencing a series of dramatic UFO encounters.

This family experienced repeated and ongoing encounters with metallic craft that landed less than fifty feet from their home. However, these encounters were more than just sightings, more properly qualified as close encounters of the fourth kind. There are strong indications that communication occurred between the witnesses and the UFO occupants.

In other words, contact was made.

5

Contact!

In 1991, ROGER and Sarah
Martin moved into Topanga with their young son.
Sarah had lived in the canyon many years before and
was overjoyed to move with her family into their own
home. They found a nice house located in the center of
the canyon, up Entrada, near Topanga State Park.

Roger works as a landscaper. Sarah is employed as a
flight attendant.

On Saturday, June 20, 1992, at around 2:45 A.M.,
Sarah was awakened from a very strange dream.
Awake, she saw a large object hovering outside her
bedroom window. The object was covered with brightly colored lights, and made a low buzzing noise.

She knew instantly that she was seeing something
very strange. "I sat up in bed and looked out my window and there were these bright lights outside, but
not shining into my room. And there's a tree in front
of my window; so at first glance, I thought it was a
car in the street, going down the street. But it wasn't.

51

It was in the field across from my house. And it was a ship!

"It wasn't humongous; it was just about the size of two or three cars put end-to-end, like mid-sized cars. And it was about twenty feet off the ground. And it was just sitting there, no noise except that hum. I woke Roger up, he looked, and the thing left. I mean, it went up and out and forward; it did all those things at the same time . . . I mean, it was gone. And I walked outside to look at the sky, and I couldn't find it."

Although she only saw the object briefly, it was so large and close that it was virtually impossible to mis-perceive. And yet, it was so strange Sarah had difficulty describing it. "It was all lit up like a Christmas tree . . . it was solid. It was a craft. It was a ship. It looked to me like a saucer, but it looked cylindrical. I mean, it looked to me like a cylinder, yet it was a saucer. I think from one point of view it looks like a saucer, and from another point of view, if you looked at if from the front, it would maybe be more cylinder-shaped."

Sarah noticed that there were odd window-like panels on the outside of the object. She could also clearly see colored lights moving strangely around its base. They kind of flowed into each other . . . the blue-green-purple type, the red-purple type and the white-yellow type . . . the lights were not continually one light. They were mixed together."

The object was also resting on an opaque beam of white-yellow light. As Sarah continued, "The white light came from underneath. It didn't shoot out from above or the same place where those other lights were. It was underneath it, in-between the object and the ground. It was on the ground, but yet it was so bright that it wasn't even aimed for my house but it came towards this direction . . . it reflected. It was very bright."

Sarah also noticed another important detail. Like many other Topanga UFO witnesses, she heard a strange humming noise. "You could hear it, but it wasn't an irritating hum . . . you know when you get close to a transformer box and you hear that sound of electricity going through? It was like that, yet different. It was almost musical. I think you might have heard it like . . . after a piano's been played, the reverberation from it afterwards, the note hanging on. Only this was a continuous thing . . . [a] humming sound . . . like nothing . . . I've ever heard before."

Sarah was also deeply impressed by the sudden and total lack of animal noises while the object was present. "We have owls and all kinds of animals and dogs and everything—totally quiet. Not one cricket . . . like the animals know something's going on."

Everything about the object was strange. Even the way it moved seemed unexplainable. Not only did it hover on a beam of light, but it left instantaneously. As Sarah says, "Now, this sounds really strange too, but the way it flies is not possible as described in our dimension. It is impossible to maneuver the way that this thing flies. It went out, up and gone. It's impossible with the way that we travel for anything to move that fast. It was gone in seconds, out of view from the whole canyon." The object Sarah saw was so strange, there is no way it could have been mistaken for a helicopter or other conventional craft.

The next morning, they inspected the ground where the object had hovered. There were no burns, no depressions, no marks—nothing to indicate that a large metallic object had hovered there only hours earlier.

The lack of evidence was upsetting, but what most concerned Sarah was the motive behind the encounter. Why was it hovering right outside their bedroom window? Sarah believes that, whatever the reason, it has something to do with the strange dream she was having just prior to the encounter.

In the dream, Sarah clearly remembered being inside a strange white room, surrounded by even stranger beings. It was only with reluctance that Sarah admitted that she believed the dream was probably more than just a dream.

"I've tried to think about it quite a bit actually, and tried to remember every little thing. But to be honest with you, and I know this sounds really strange, I have a feeling that I was out of my body for that dream . . . I believe I was in the ship . . . I believe that I was actually having an out-of-body experience, and what woke me up was when I came back into my body. And I believe that's why they were so close to my house."

Unknown to Sarah, many other people have reported similar experiences. During her "dream," however, Sarah was told several things by the beings. They even gave her predictions, one of which may have already come true.

At the time of the experience, the 1992 presidential campaign was in full force. Sarah was a strong supporter of Ross Perot. She tried to convince everyone she knew to vote for Ross Perot as the next President of the United States. As time went on, she found herself becoming more and more politically active.

But then came the encounter.

Sarah described her "dream" in her own words: "I was in a white room with . . . things. That's where I have a problem. To be honest with you, I can't remember their faces. I just remember talking to them, and I was in a white room. A white room, I remember that. And they were talking to me. And this is what they said: 'Why are you so involved in this campaign? Why are you wasting your time? It's going to fall apart, one by one, and whoever wins, it doesn't matter because the whole system is going to come down around everybody. And there's going to be a rebellion. And you're not a part of this, so don't get involved.'"

"I was so petrified when I woke up," Sarah continued, "that I couldn't sleep for the rest of the night. I can't sleep in my bedroom anymore. I sleep in the living room, on the floor, away from the window."

Sarah had dreams before, but this was totally unlike a dream. As she said, "This was so incredible. In my mind, I keep going over again what they said: 'You're not a part of this, so don't be a part of it. Get away from all of it.' I understand what they mean, and I think in time, I will be able to. The other thing too is something about an earthquake, a big earthquake. Something like that, but that's not the thing that stuck out the most. The thing that stuck out the most was, 'Why are you so involved? Why are you letting this consume your time? It's not worth it, and it's all going to fall apart.'"

Sarah couldn't help but be impressed by the experience. Unknown to her, many other UFO witnesses have been told similar stories of future disasters and even the dangers of political involvement. The experience was even more real when Sarah woke up to see the object right outside her house. "They were repeating it over and over again: 'You're not a part of this. You're not a part of this. So don't—' So it was like they were brainwashing me in one way."

"The minute I was conscious of something, I don't know what it was, I was back in my body. I sat straight up in bed, looked straight out my window. I got up on my knees, looked out my window, and that's when I saw it. Now, I know what I know, and that's just what it was. And there was something tying that dream with that ship. And I don't know how they do it. I don't know what they . . . all I know is that they weren't there to hurt me. They were just telling me some stuff. I don't know what it means. Well I know what it means, but I don't know why they were telling me. I don't know what I have to do with the whole situation."

Sarah, like many other people who have similar experiences, feels an urgency to tell other people what the beings told her. "Is there anybody else I can talk to about this? Because it's like I have a message or something. I don't know what it is; it's just really weird."

The message given to Sarah is very clear. Humanity's future is very uncertain. Sarah remarked, "Mark my words, I think things are really going to get nasty in this country in the next couple of years. And I think that's what they're saying. And I think that they mean if you're a part of it, you're a part of the problem . . .

That's the thing I got from this dream. We are in a hell of a mess, and apparently, this is a course that is supposed to be happening. I don't know."

Sarah's husband, Roger, didn't see or hear the object that night, and the story his wife told him was so strange, he couldn't help but be skeptical. Still he could tell that something had upset his wife. But a spaceship?

Both were also concerned about another detail: Sarah was, at the time, pregnant. In fact, she was having a very unusual pregnancy. She was originally pregnant with twins; however, one of the fetuses died in utero. She was told by her doctor that the chances of carrying the other child to full term were extremely slim.

So when the object appeared, Sarah felt instant concern for her unborn baby. However, as she said, "I don't believe they were trying to harm me. I believe that it was just me out of this body. I don't think it had anything to do with the baby. However, I do believe, and I get the feeling, that they are coming around to check on me. And this is really bizarre. I have no idea why they would come around to check on me being pregnant."

From that day on, Sarah stopped her political involvement. The next day she met her girlfriends for lunch and told them the whole story. She told her friends simply, "I'm done. I don't want to be a part of it anymore."

Sarah went from political activist to withdrawing completely from politics. As she said, "The day before, I couldn't do enough. I couldn't talk to enough people about Perot. I had the dream and boom, that was it."

Roger was less concerned about his wife's political affiliations and more concerned about her physical health. Could the object have had something to do with her unusual pregnancy? Roger asked Sarah, "What if they think there's something really special?"

Sarah could only reply, "I don't know." Sarah does feel that the UFO occupants are friendly. "Let me just tell you, the other night, being conscious like that, they weren't hurting me. They were just telling me the way things were going to be. And they were trying to prepare me for something. . . . It was a very good experience, but it's still frightening because you don't know exactly . . . what about the time I wasn't conscious in that thing? What was happening then? Was that just my body? Did they zap me? You know, you get all these kinds of questions. Was I physically in there or was my soul in there?"

The next day, they discussed the encounter and decided that Sarah must have seen a UFO. Whether or not she was actually inside, they are not certain. Sarah does feel that there was definitely a contact involving communication.

Both of them, however, assumed that it was a once-in-a-lifetime event. After all, neither of them had ever thought about UFOs before, much less seen one. They had no reason to suspect that the experiences would continue.

Actually, their experiences were just beginning. Over the next few months, Roger and Sarah Martin would experience a series of encounters that would turn their world upside down. As time went on, one fact would become increasingly clear; for some reason, the objects were very interested in them.

The next night, at around 3:00 A.M., Roger was awakened by a strange buzzing sound. He then noticed that all the animal sounds outside had stopped. It was completely quiet, except for the buzzing.

He leaned forward, looked out his bedroom window, and received the shock of his life. Less than fifty feet away a giant, metallic-looking, disk-shaped craft had landed in a field. The object glowed with an eerie violet-blue light, and sat next to the road in full view of several houses. It was in the exact same spot that Sarah had seen it the night before.

Roger expected the craft to take off right away, but to his surprise, the thing remained. He soon realized that, whatever the object was, it wasn't going away any time soon.

Because he saw it so closely, Roger was able to provide a very clear description of the object (see Figure 1).

Figure 1: Relative sizes of objects Roger Martin sighted.
(Based on sketches by witness)

"I don't want to say cigar-shaped because I've heard that before, but it's elongated with a kind of domed top. It's inverted on the sides and then it goes . . . I'd have to sketch it for you to get a really good idea of what it looks like exactly, but it seemed something very streamlined. That's why I didn't say cigar-shaped. It's very streamlined and it had inverted sides on it. And as far as all the lights, I hear a lot of people talking about lights and stuff like this, but this was illumination. It wasn't what would be lights *per se,* you know, how you would see a round light? This was illumination across the whole kind of metallic-looking framework of it—a blue and purplish type of light. And they are very strange because they're not like regular lights as far as what I was explaining to you, round lights. It's like a strip of illumination that goes around the circumference of the vehicle, or ship, or whatever you'd call it. And whatever it's being propelled by is very cool and quiet. Because I know exactly where they landed and I came over to the field and looked. And there are no charred marks. I've heard things where the grass is charred and stuff like this. I don't know what kind of radioactivity's going on over there or anything like that, but the grass is virtually unscathed. There was no dirt dug out or anything like that. I've been over there and checked several times."

As he stared at the object, Roger was surprised that it didn't leave. He thought of waking Sarah, but remembering how upset she had been the night before, he decided against it. Instead he continued quietly observing the craft, noting all the details. The more he looked, the more he was impressed by the strangeness of the craft. For example he, like Sarah, saw strange panels on the side of the craft. As he said, "They're not even like windows; they're more like panels. And it seems you'd think it's metallic, but there's no shine to it, so it seems like a non-metallic finish on it. I don't know. It's very similar to KEVLAR®, something like that. But it's a very bland color, very bland, not silver, but not completely gray either. It's odd. I mean, I made some sketches of it and it really just blew my mind. The night after I saw it, I drew it."

After twenty minutes had passed, Roger wondered what was going on. Why wouldn't the object leave? What was it doing just sitting there? These questions and others raced through his mind. Twenty minutes turned into a half-hour, and still the object just sat there, unmoving. Roger stared wide-awake, quietly observing, trying not to get too scared. As he lay watching the craft, it suddenly occurred to him that the object knew very well that he was watching it.

He thought of going outside, but fear of what could happen kept him in his bed. Roger describes how he felt as he gazed upon the object. "I don't know what's going on and I hear about that lost time stuff and things like that. I looked at it this way. They're coming here; there's a reason. Their technology is higher than ours. . . . If I was going to come to some other planet, I'd be taking specimens, and I'd be checking them out. Who knows if I'd release them or not? If I was doing it in a scientific way, is what I'm saying. And I know if I was an explorer, I'd be very interested too. So what their motives are, who knows? So I'm not just going to go out there and go crazy. But I was gazing at it, and they obviously knew I was there. They are a very highly intelligent life, whatever's going on."

So in the interests of not becoming a specimen himself, Roger remained inside. After a total of forty-five minutes, Roger was simply unable to stay up any longer. So despite the fact that the craft was still there, Roger surprised himself by falling asleep. When he awoke the next morning, the object was gone.

As soon as Sarah awoke, Roger told her what happened. This time, Sarah noticed that Roger was extremely upset. He was very protective of her and was worried that the object was interested in them for some reason.

His fears seemed to be validated when the object returned again the very next night. But this time, it was a different kind of object.

Again, around 3:30 A.M., Roger woke up, looked out his window and saw an object hovering over the same spot. But this time it was a small disk-shaped object, a mere ten-feet in diameter (see Figure 1). It was hovering a few feet up in the air, making a soft, buzzing noise. Again, all normal outside sounds had ceased, and Roger stared at the object in total amazement. He recalled, "The second time I saw it, it was a different vehicle. It was a different ship completely . . . it was almost like a flying disk, very similar. The details were: it's very saucer-like with the inverted sides on it. It's hard to describe. The bottom's flat, and then when you come over the bottom flatness, it inverts and then it comes to almost like a dome with it semi-flattened on top. So it was very, very strange. Really weird-looking."

Again Roger didn't wake Sarah, and continued to watch the disk. Again there were no visible lights on the craft, and yet it glowed with a violet-blue illumination. Roger was mostly impressed by the small size of the craft. He estimated it had a diameter of no more than ten feet and a height of four feet. It hovered in the sky about fifteen feet above the ground.

Just when he was wondering if it was ever going to leave, the object darted away at high speed. As Roger said, "It was there about fifteen minutes, and it left so fast, I can't tell you how fast—like you blinked your eyes and it was gone . . . it whizzed off quite rapidly."

The next morning, Roger told Sarah what happened. They were amazed, but by now, they were getting used to it. They told their friends. A few of Roger's friends also admitted to having seen UFOs over Topanga Canyon.

Around this time, the *Messenger* article came out. Sarah happened to glance at the paper and see the article. After reading it, she immediately called the *Messenger* and filed a report. Both she and Roger were amazed that so many other people had been seeing the UFOs. Whatever was happening, they weren't alone.

The next night, Roger and Sarah went to bed not knowing what to expect. The previous three nights had been quite eventful. That evening, however, the objects failed to appear. The night after that was also uneventful. As the days slowly passed, Roger and Sarah began to breathe more easily. The UFOs, it seemed, were gone for good.

However, the UFOs were just taking a short break. A whole new series of dramatic encounters would soon take place.

These new encounters began about two weeks after the last encounter. It was Independence Day, and Roger's brother, James, came to pick up Roger and take them to a Fourth of July party. It was around 8:00 P.M. as they drove northward along Topanga Canyon Boulevard. The traffic was light, with only a few other cars passing in the other direction.

As they headed towards the valley, Roger decided to tell James about the objects. He started with Sarah's story and then described how the objects returned for the next two nights.

Roger could tell that James was stunned by the story. As Roger continued, he could tell that his brother found it harder to believe. He began to regret sharing his story, afraid that James would react badly. James finally told Roger that he just couldn't believe that aliens were visiting Topanga Canyon, much less his own family. Roger simply replied, "Well, listen, I don't really either, but you can't dispute what I saw."

About two miles before the Top o' Topanga, they argued about whether or not UFOs were real, when they both immediately saw a strange object hovering on the opposite side of the canyon, less than a mile away. Roger noticed immediately that the object was not only strange-looking. It was huge! And it was hovering, unmoving.

Both of them stared at it in stunned silence. As Roger said, "This is really strange, but we saw a craft like nothing we saw before. And these were all visible red lights. It was a large craft moving very slowly. It wasn't a blimp; it wasn't anything like this . . . this was just really low flying, just above the trees."

Although it was the Fourth of July, they never even considered that they were seeing fireworks. They were looking at obviously some sort of craft. In fact, Roger could see many lights situated in strange places all over it. "It must have had fifteen to twenty red lights on it. I don't know. It could have been something that was just going, but we've never seen anything fly like that. It was really strange." Neither Roger nor James could believe their eyes. There were other cars on the road, but nobody else seemed to even notice the huge blimp-like object.

Roger continued driving as the large object glided south down the canyon and disappeared into one of the smaller canyons. He estimated that the sighting lasted a total of about thirty seconds, enough to convince him that the UFOs were still in Topanga.

By now, Roger was getting used to seeing the objects. James, on the other hand, had never seen one before. He had been puzzled and confused by Roger's story, but his own sighting affected him in a deeper way. He turned to Roger and said simply, "Wow, that was weird." He now takes UFOs reports much more seriously.

Although his brother was awestruck, Roger took the experience in stride. A few nights later, Roger and Sarah were asleep when the object came back again. This time, however, Roger couldn't see it and Sarah refused to even look.

They knew the object was around because all animal sounds had ceased and a strange humming buzz sound was easily heard. As Roger said, "There have been times I haven't seen them, but I know they're around. There's this really—it's weird, nothing that we hear normally, this weird kind of humming sound. You know when someone has a really loud refrigerator, that kind of humming? It's similar to that, but more intense. It's definitely more intense."

As July progressed, Roger and Sarah would hear the familiar hum of the object at least twice a week. Because of Sarah's pregnancy, they had no desire to go UFO hunting, and wished the encounters would stop. It was around this time that Sarah began sleeping in the living room, away from the bedroom window.

Sometime early in the second week of July, an incredible event occurred. In fact, of all Roger's experiences, it was the one that impressed him most.

It started when Roger again awakened in the early morning hours to the familiar buzzing sound of the object. He sat up, wondering if he would see the giant forty-foot craft or the small ten-foot craft. Instead, he realized that the buzzing sound was different. In fact, it sounded more like a car, specifically a Volkswagen Beetle. Relieved, he was just about to lay down and go back to sleep when he saw the car drive by. Hovering a mere ten feet above the car was a small, metallic disk, about ten feet wide and four feet high. The craft was actually following the car as it sped up the road. The entire area around the car was illuminated by the purple light of the object.

Roger could barely believe his eyes. "The weirdest one was when I just woke up because I heard a Volkswagen with a really strange noise also, like a loud sputtering Volkswagen coming up the hill. And I looked out my window, and right above it was a very small craft, which is a lot different from the ones I see normally. And it was hovering above it and following it up the hill, quite silently, a weird hum almost . . . it was a loud Volkswagen, but with a weird humming sound. And I recognized this humming sound. So I got up and looked, and I thought, 'Oh, it's just a Volkswagen,' And then fifteen feet above this Volkswagen, maybe ten feet, it was following this Volkswagen up the street. I mean, that's weird. And if you see how these things fly, you can't describe it. It's like nothing you've seen fly. It's remarkable the agility it has. It just hovers and smoothly, I mean, like the thing could do almost anything."

Roger lay there, stunned. Did the people in the Volkswagen know they were being chased? Roger doesn't know. The car didn't seem to be speeding. On the other hand, the disk was so low, it was practically on top of the car. It lit up the whole area in purple-blue light. It was the only time Roger ever saw the disk arrive. As he recalled, "I'd never seen it arrive. The only time I'd ever seen anything coming was the time when I woke up and looked out my window and it was following that Volkswagen down the street. And I don't know how the Volkswagen didn't see it. I don't know if anyone reported it or anything. But it was kind of strange. It was just above the wires, the telephone wires, following. It was illuminating the street."

Unfortunately, Roger has no idea who the driver was, and as of yet, no one has stepped forward. The experience shows, however, that the Topanga UFOs have a propensity towards chasing people in their cars. It wasn't the first such incident, and I would later investigate others.

Meanwhile, Roger and Sarah continued to have encounters. All this UFO activity began to draw the attention of other Topanga residents. At least four more people joined the ranks of Topanga Canyon eyewitnesses. Furthermore, the sightings had taken a new twist. They were becoming predictable. The objects were returning so often and with such regularity, that Roger and Sarah could predict when they would appear.

6

They Return

On the night of July 14, 1992, the UFOs returned.

Less than two miles away from Roger and Sarah's house, another couple was preparing their home for guests. The guests were Phillip and Mandy, the same couple who had witnessed UFOs over Topanga Canyon one month earlier. The other couple, Jonathan and Susan, was also the same couple who had entertained Phillip and Mandy in their home up on Entrada.

Jonathan and Susan have lived in Topanga for decades, and are very familiar with the area. For the past couple of weeks, another couple, Anthony and Emily, were also staying at Jonathan and Susan's house.

That evening after dinner, the couples decided to go for a walk into the state park. After changing into some warmer clothes, Susan, Anthony, Phillip, and Mandy all got in the car and parked near the entrance to the park.

They quietly walked up one of the many trails that criss-cross the park. Susan led everyone to a particularly nice spot in the park.

Anthony is a UFO contactee. He has had many experiences with UFOs and extraterrestrials who call themselves the Pleiadians. On many occasions, Anthony has received telepathic messages from UFOs. They have even told him to be in a certain place at a certain time, and he would see the UFOs.

On this particular evening, Anthony was taking the group out for the specific purpose of seeing a UFO.

The four of them sat in a circle and meditated. At about 11:00 P.M., they became tired and decided to leave. As they walked down the path, Phillip noticed a star-like light moving in the sky above their heads. At first he thought that his eyes were causing the star to appear to move—a phenomenon known as auto-kinesis. But when he looked at the other stars, none of them appeared to move. When Phillip looked back at the original "star," it was still moving.

As Phillip said, "I thought at first I might have been looking at a satellite. We had just taken a hike out in the park there, and we were hiking back. And I kind of tipped my head up and looked way up in the sky. And jokingly I said, 'Wow, look at that. That's a moving star. That could be a UFO.' And I watched it for a while, and I thought it was just a satellite tracking across the sky. But then it started moving in a circular pattern. And I said, 'Wait a minute. This is not a satellite.' But that's when I said, 'Hey, folks. I think this might be a UFO up here." And I watched it move. It moved around in a circular pattern."

Anthony followed where Phillip pointed and immediately saw the object. There was no doubt in his mind that it was very strange. "I didn't spot it first. I forget who it was, but it was unusual . . . all the stars were going one way and this thing was going the other way, and it was sort of—let me see if I can get this straight— it was basically wiggling. It was wiggling and moving opposite to the stars. I mean, the stars were going in one direction and this was wiggling and going the other way. It stopped and wiggled some more, and stopped and wiggled some more, and just kept on going contrary to the stars. But it wasn't a meteorite that could do that. Meteorites just go across."

Like Phillip, Anthony thought at first that his eyes were causing the movement, but the longer he watched, the more he realized it couldn't be a star. As he said, "It moved contrary to the stars. The stars would move very slowly in one direction. This thing was moving almost the opposite direction. It would stop, it would wiggle. And by wiggle, I thought maybe, you know how you move your head and things wiggle? I thought it was one of those things."

Aside from the object moving opposite to the stars, Anthony noticed other strange details. One was the vivid colors that came from the object. "The colors were interesting in that they were different colors than the rest of the stars. It was a more bluish-white color. It was very bluish-white."

Phillip's wife Mandy remembers there being several star-like objects moving around. She was totally amazed by what she saw. "That night, that was absolutely marvelous. There was more than one just moving around.

There were stars in formation doing the most amazing dance. That was truly remarkable, truly remarkable. We were on a moonlight walk back from a big oak tree, and all of a sudden we looked up and there were, God—I can't even tell you how many, ten stars that were just dancing around in circles in the sky. It was absolutely beautiful. They were just going off in all these different directions, then coming back together again. [It was] extremely obvious. There were too many of them. There were too many of us up there who saw them. Was it just the four of us? Anthony, Susan, Phillip, and me. But it wasn't like there was just one of them. There were numbers of them. I'm guessing at least ten, but maybe even more. But I wasn't counting, I was so flabbergasted. It was beautiful, absolutely beautiful. And it was like they knew we were out there. We'd actually gone for a long meditation under this tree, and as we were walking back, it was like they were saying hello and letting us know that they were there, and just enjoying the contact. It was joyful."

Susan was quietly and carefully observing the events as they unfolded. She remembers the night very well. "We were gazing at the stars in the sky and one of the people looked up and saw one of the stars. Though we all identified it as a star because it looked to be in about the same caliber of brightness and about the same distance away, it appeared to be moving. And not the kind of movement that you would experience as stars are blinking, and as you focus on them that your retina begins to see things just slightly change positions. This star-like object was moving in such a way that, as I recall, it was going in a large circle, and it would sometimes disappear and would appear in a different place. And this is all in a very, very small segment of space.

"And there were four of us," Susan continued, "standing with our necks craned and heads looking straight above us. And this object, this star-like light, would flash. And it would flash these long flashes of light off to one side, as if it were some kind of beacon. The flash itself wasn't very big, and I can't remember if there were any colors or not."

Further evidence that the object was not a star came when all four of them simultaneously saw it move. As Susan said, "There were a couple of times when we would all call out, 'Oh, did you see that?' or 'Oh, look at that!' because it was doing these things. It might be one person who would say, 'Gee, did you see that flash? Did you see that change direction?' or 'Did you see it blink?' But when several of us saw it at the same time and would articulate what we saw, we began to think, 'Well, maybe this is not a star.' Because the other stars that were around this object were not doing the same thing."

Mandy also remembers the thrill of corroboration. She said, "We just stood out there. We couldn't believe it. We just couldn't believe it. It was so much fun. We all kept saying, 'Are you seeing this?' 'Yeah, I'm seeing this.' 'Did you see that one over there?' 'Yes.' 'Is that the one that just turned the loop?' 'Yes.' It was like they were pretending they were stars, and then all of a sudden, Anthony kind of directed our attention up. And he said something like, 'They're here.' I can't remember what he said exactly, but it was something like that. And we all looked up. And then it was like the show began. And they all at once just started dancing and moving around in the sky. And before that, they'd been very still and they looked like stars."

After about twenty minutes of observing the objects, the witnesses tired of watching them. Anthony had experienced much more dramatic sightings and wasn't particularly impressed by this one. He knows from experience that these types of sightings are actually quite common. As he said, "It wasn't that fantastic a sighting because pretty much if you sit out at night and you lie on your back, you will see quite a bit of wiggling and things doing stuff like that. I feel that they are there pretty much regularly. But it's hard to say if it's a regular occurrence or just a special occurrence. It wasn't really that much of a fantastic sighting. After a while it gets very tiring to be looking up at this wiggling thing in the sky. We didn't stay there for more than a half-hour."

Later that evening, after her guests had departed, Susan checked to see if the object was still there. Unfortunately, she was not able to locate exactly where the object had been.

Although the above sighting was quite distant, the fact that it occurred over Topanga is significant. What's even more significant, however, is that at the time of the sighting, Roger and Sarah Martin were in the middle of what would turn out to be the busiest month yet for UFOs.

Two days before the previous encounter, on July 12, Roger and Sarah were again visited by the object. Usually Roger awakened around 3:00 A.M. by the sound of the buzzing around his house. It was during

July, however, that he began to notice that he was waking up before the object actually arrived. His wife had told him about her initial dream, which she felt represented some type of communication with the object. He wondered, could this be happening to him?

Said Roger, "I've also noticed that there's something else besides just hearing them or seeing lights and things like that. There's some kind of communication through us. I mean, I wake up automatically. It wakes me up before [the animals] even hear something going on too, so it's very strange."

Roger is also unable to explain the complete lack of animal sounds. "I know that the animals are really in tune to it . . . the animals just—it's almost like they just shut off. And you know how noisy they are. You have the crickets, the owls, coyotes yipping all night. It's a very loud nature sound and it goes on constantly all night long. And when [the objects are] around, it's quiet. It's dead, deafening silence, that's what it's like. I mean, the dogs don't bark. There's nothing. No crickets, nothing. And I find that very odd . . . the wildlife around here, they don't lie. When something weird's going on, they don't just shut down for no reason."

On July 14, when Roger awoke and heard the buzzing noise and the animal sounds quiet down, he knew that the object was back again. He looked outside, but saw nothing unusual. His wife, however, was sleeping alone in the living room. He jumped up and went to check on her.

Sarah was already awake, listening to the strange buzzing noise. She hid under the blanket, obviously upset that the object had returned.

Roger said to her, "They're here."

"I know they are," Sarah replied.

"What do you want to do?"

"Let's just both sleep together."

They both went into the bedroom and laid in bed. The buzzing sound was still audible so they stayed up and talked, trying to ignore the sound. After about a half-hour, Roger said, "Here comes a car."

To their surprise, the car seemed to chase the object away. Sarah said, "We could hear a car coming, and after the car went by, there wasn't the hum anymore."

Outside, the animal noises began again, and Roger and Sarah were able to go back to sleep. Still, they were really beginning to wonder why the object was showing so much interest in them.

Sarah was upset by the encounter and she could tell that it also upset Roger. She said, "He's very protective, especially of me right now, because of the things happening. I've got to tell you, he was really wigged out the other night when he thought they were back and I was in the other room by myself . . . ."

A few days later, the object was back again. This time, however, Roger was able to see it. In fact, the object returned for three consecutive nights.

It began in the usual way, with Roger waking up at about 3:00 A.M. Then the outside sounds quieted and the familiar buzzing noise filled the air. Sometimes when this occurred, Roger would look outside and see nothing. Other times, an object was clearly visible. After about fifteen minutes, the buzzing sound would usually stop, and the sounds outside would resume, or Roger would simply fall back asleep. Rarely did he ever see the object leave.

On this occasion, when Roger looked out the window, he saw a giant metallic-looking craft, glowing with an unearthly light.

As Roger said, "All the crickets, the animals, no noise, which is kind of strange. Then that weird, strange humming of the vehicle would wake me up . . . each time I would look up, they'd be there. And you know, I was scared to even go out. I would've gone out there, but you know, I don't know what their motives are. It just really freaks you out when you see something like that."

Because he works as a landscaper, Roger often comes home exhausted. Each time that he was awakened by the object, he was so tired that he was physically unable to keep an all-night vigil.

He admitted that it is strange he always falls asleep before the objects leave. He also remarked that he has never seen the larger-sized object leave. "Every time I've seen the long one, I've never seen it really leave. I've heard it leave before, but I've never sat there and watched it. Because it's pretty bizarre. It's pretty big sitting over there, and I don't know if they're watching me or [what's] going on."

By now, Roger was getting quite used to seeing the objects. Sarah, however, was becoming increasingly concerned. Sleeping in the living room didn't prevent the objects from waking her up. Unlike Roger, she refuses to even so much as look outside. Because of this, she has not seen the objects as many times as Roger has.

She wished the encounters would stop. "I still think it's around because we still wake up in the middle of the night hearing the hum . . . we really don't want to engage in any activity with it, especially with my pregnancy, and this is unknown territory. I don't know what they're going to do. I don't want to risk anything to my baby. I mean, this is kind of scary because I have heard tales of other things, people being abducted and everything like that. I don't want to be involved in anything like that. It was strange enough that they were by my house and I had that dream."

Sarah was even more upset because in her dream, she was told not to be politically active because the whole system would fall apart. Sarah had stopped supporting the Perot candidacy and just waited to see what would happen. To her surprise, Perot dropped out of the race. This simple fact seemed to verify what she was told in the dream. As Sarah said, "What does that tell you? That is almost like predicting the future, and that kind of freaked me out that they would tell me that three weeks [previously]. I am just so crazed by this whole thing . . . And I can't wait to see what else happens now. To be honest with you, with my pregnancy and everything, I just want to kind of stay away from all of it."

However, the very next night the object came again. Roger awoke and saw that the craft was hovering in its usual spot, right next to the road, in full view of several houses. Again, the object showed no signs of movement. Roger, already exhausted, fell back asleep.

The next day he told Sarah what happened. They both wondered if it would be back again the next night. They had noticed that the sightings seemed to come in clusters. Nearly a month previously, the first encounters occurred for three days in a row. So both of them knew that there was a strong possibility that the UFOs would be back again the next night.

Sure enough, at about 3:00 A.M. the next night, Roger was again awoken. He looked out the window, and this time, he saw the smaller disk-shaped craft. As usual, it was hovering several feet above the ground. As soon as Roger looked at it, it darted away. "When I got up to look at the thing," he said. "It didn't stay there for more than ten, fifteen, twenty seconds. And then, the small one just went—shew! It was the small one."

Both Roger and Sarah were not surprised that the object had returned. It was almost as if they were following some kind of schedule. They realized that they could almost predict when the objects would arrive. As Roger related, "I think that if somebody came up there and hung out, he or she would see them. Three o'clock in the morning. Anywhere from one to three. They're here. They're around . . . I definitely believe they're here for a reason. I don't know what it is."

Sarah, like Roger, began to notice patterns in the visits. She also suspected that the UFOs were, in fact, interested in her pregnancy. "Why is it that they keep coming back? It's like they're checking up on my pregnancy . . . it's a feeling I have, and my feelings are usually not too far off. I feel like they come by about twice a week and check on me."

Although the encounters scare her, Sarah has repeatedly stated that the objects are by no means hostile. As she says, "I'm not feeling bad about it. I'm just a little nervous. This is not an everyday happening for me. I don't see these types of things . . . actually, it really was kind of exciting."

Both Roger and Sarah were also surprised that all of Topanga wasn't talking about the UFOs. Something like this, they thought, should be attracting a lot of attention.

Actually, unknown to either of them, the number of witnesses was growing exponentially. In fact, the UFOs were so active, they were attracting more attention than either of them realized.

In many UFO flap areas, agencies of the United States federal government take an interest in the activity. Investigators and witnesses of UFO flap areas may find that they themselves become targets of investigation. Unmarked black helicopters are frequently reported.[1]

All through July, the Topanga Canyon UFOs returned at least twice a week. In mid-July they returned for three nights in a row. Roger and Sarah were able to predict the sightings simply because they were occurring with such regularity.

As it turned out, Roger and Sarah were not the only people expecting the UFOs to arrive. On one of the nights during the middle of the visitations, Roger was awoken, not by the objects, but by the sound of a large military-type helicopter hovering over the area, shining down a beam of light, as if searching for something.

Not only was it unusual for such a large helicopter to be searching the area so late at night, but it was even more unusual that the helicopter stayed for such a long time.

As Roger reported, "I don't know if it's the military. I know what the new police choppers sound like, but these, they're larger. They're more like jet-prop heli-copters. They search this area a lot and I don't know why that is. Because it's not like a regular police one just doing rounds . . . There have been a few nights where they've been hovering over here for literally hours in the middle of the night. So I don't know if they're tracking it, the military, or whatever they're doing."

Roger saw only one helicopter in the sky at a time, and he was unable to discern any markings on the side. The sound of the helicopter reminded him of the new Coast Guard helicopters which, although still loud, are sixty percent quieter than conventional helicopters. Roger explained, "They go really fast. Those are the ones they are using. The rear rotor is all concealed. They're really neat choppers. Those are the ones they are using to hover over this area. And it's too late for me to get any insignia on the side or anything like that, but it's pretty bizarre. And the one time they were hovering for hours that night, those were the days when [the UFOs] were coming. So that's why I tied that in somehow . . . it was when they were around . . . they were searching the area like crazy. I don't know if someone called and said they saw something out there, or what was going on, but they were there for a long time that night."

Roger was not the only one to complain of the unusual helicopter activity. Another Topanga resident, who lives a few miles across the canyon also noticed the helicopters and was actually kept awake by the noise. It was on the same night, and like Roger he also wondered "what the heck was going on."

It is well-known that the military is deeply interested in UFOs, and the Topanga Canyon encounters seem to be no exception. Unmarked helicopters harassing witnesses have become an increasing problem. Later on, I uncovered further evidence that the military or some agency of the federal government was deeply involved in studying the Topanga Canyon UFO encounters.

Meanwhile, Roger and Sarah continued to be visited regularly by the humming objects. By the time July was over, Roger and Sarah had had so many encounters that they were having trouble keeping the dates straight. But when the objects came back again the week of August 12–17, it became clear there was a pattern to the encounters.

The pattern was firmly established by the encounters of the previous two months. As Roger related, "Actually it's pretty frequent, about three times a month. And they usually come back to back. They usually come three days in a row, so I don't know what that's for . . . you know, I could pattern them because it's strange—there is a pattern, but it's not super-consistent. I can't tell you why; because they were coming really consistently for a while and then stopped coming . . . it would be almost a month apart every time. I only saw it three days in a row for each of those months."

So when August rolled around and the objects showed up, Roger was not really surprised. As usual, he woke up, noticed the absence of animal sounds, and heard the low buzzing noise. He looked outside, and as he expected, there was the object. Eventually he returned to sleep.

The next night, the same thing happened. The third night was yet another repeat performance. By this time,

Roger was getting tired of the visitations. As he says, "I looked up at it once or twice. And I even heard it the third time. I didn't get up after that because I just knew it was there, and what am I going to do?"

Roger knows that for most people, seeing a UFO would be extremely interesting, and he doesn't take the experience lightly. He has even taken to keeping a camera by his bedside in the hopes of getting a photograph. Part of Roger's failure to obtain a photo may be because he is very reluctant to come forward with his story. He has no desire at all to convince anybody that UFOs are real. He was extremely reluctant to be interviewed and wants no publicity at all. Both he and Sarah prefer to just get on with their lives. And although the UFOs aren't hostile in any way, the constant visits cause them some concern. As Roger said, "It's pretty bizarre. It's really eerie when it happens. I don't know what it is. Whatever's going on, I don't want to egg them on and go out there."

After August, the encounters seemed to slow down. Occasionally, however, Roger and Sarah would again be awoken by the sound of the object hovering outside. By this time Roger knew exactly what to listen for. " . . . first . . . is the [silence in the] woods , because you're not always going to hear them come. Sometimes they are just there. And then it starts, a really weird humming, a really weird sound, a kind of haunting sound. And then everything's quiet. It's weird. I mean, it doesn't happen out here like that. It's really noisy out there . . . The crickets are just going like crazy, and it's really loud."

Now that the visits have slowed, the big question for Roger and Sarah is "why?" Why did the UFOs visit them? Why did they give Sarah a message to be less politically active? Why did the UFOs come so often? Why did they stop?

Sarah has stated her feeling that it was as if the UFOs were checking up on her. Both Roger and Sarah were vaguely aware of the phenomenon of UFO abduction, in which people are taken aboard UFOs and given physical examinations. Unknown to either of them, however, many abductees report that the UFO occupants often show a tremendous interest in human reproduction.

Could it be that the UFOs were interested in Sarah because of her unusual pregnancy? When I first spoke with her, she expressed this very concern, and asked if there were any reports of UFOs and pregnant women.

Knowing that the objects were still appearing and that Sarah's pregnancy was guarded, I decided to not alarm her unduly. I told her that although such cases do exist, they are extremely rare. In fact, UFOs have shown a great interest in pregnant women, and there are several cases on record involving them, particularly women who are pregnant with twins and then mysteriously lose one of the fetuses. My decision to withhold the truth was because Sarah was under stress already due to her unusual pregnancy; any additional stress could be harmful.

Fortunately, Sarah carried her baby to full term and gave birth to a healthy baby boy. And it was around this time that the objects stopped appearing.

It seems clear why the Martins were visited. During their newborn's check-up, Sarah spontaneously recalled being aboard the UFO, and being examined. She believes the aliens were making sure her baby was healthy. She and Roger were pleased when he was born a happy bouncing baby boy, normal except for being precocious and remarkably psychic. Interestingly, a nurse told Sarah that her pregnancy and aminocentesis tests had been sent to a government lab, which according to the nurse, was unusual and had never actually happened before. Sarah was shocked. She had not told her doctor about the UFOs. Did he know something she didn't? She made the decision not to make an ordeal. But she began to suspect that her pregnancy was of interest to more than just the alleged aliens.

Today, the Martins are glad that the visits have ended. They do not want to see any more UFOs. They are not interested in any publicity and, in fact, shun it. They do not want to convince anybody of their experiences. They just want to get on with their lives. Unknown to the Martins, however, there were many other families in Topanga who were having remarkably similar experiences.

7

Missing Time on Grandview Drive

When the July 1992 issue of the *Messenger* was published, people were talking about the cover story that exposed the recent UFO encounters across Topanga Canyon. It was the perfect opportunity for residents to talk about their own sightings.

For many residents the article was merely interesting. But for those residents who were seeing the objects, the article provided something they were desperately seeking: confirmation of their own experiences. Although the witnesses had no doubts that they saw something strange, they were pleased to know they weren't alone. One woman, a Topanga resident for over forty years, read about the encounters and thought to herself, "Hey, this happened to me over thirty years ago!"

A few days later, her son contacted the *Messenger* and asked if they were interested in hearing her story. Another encounter came to light. Although the sighting occurred many years previous, it is without a doubt, one of the most amazing of all the Topanga Canyon UFO encounters.

First, this case did not involve a single witness who saw an unexplained light in the sky late at night, but three witnesses. Second, solid, metallic disks were sighted. And lastly, the sighting occurred in broad daylight. There are strong indications the encounter was more extensive than a simple sighting.

It began one summer afternoon in 1961 or 1962. Beverly Smith and her two daughters, Lisa, then seven years old, and Kim, then five, lived high on a ridgetop along Observation Drive. That afternoon they decided to go down to the local market. Beverly put her two children in the Volkswagon bus and headed down the hill.

The trip to the store normally took about twenty minutes. They drove to the store, picked up a few items, and began the return trip. Less than a mile away from home, their journey was suddenly interrupted.

It was Beverly who saw it first—two or three large, shiny, metallic disks hovering at about eye-level on the opposite ridge of the canyon, about a quarter-mile away, over the Entrada area. Beverly pulled up to the intersection of Observation and Grandview and parked along the side of the road. Beverly ushered her children out of the bus and instructed them to look at the objects.

"I saw these two, what we referred to then as flying saucers or whatever—outer space things. I saw these two—it's over near where the park is. It was right in there. And so, all of a sudden, they came together, and one just kind of set down and stopped . . . you could see them really clearly, and it was just really strange. They were round like the pictures you see these days— round, similar to those tops that you push and spin, the old-fashioned spinning tops. The cone was on the top. They seemed flat on the bottom." Beverly noticed that the disks were silver and glinted brightly in the late afternoon sun. She saw no lights on the object, nor did she hear any noise.

Lisa also remembers the event vividly. She is sure, however, that there were three objects, not two. She is confident her memory is correct, because she remembers that the objects were hovering in a triangular formation. "We saw these three objects in the sky, and to me, I remember them being kind of multi-colored and soft. They weren't hard-shaped things; they didn't really have distinct edges. They were saucer-shaped, but they looked diffused at the edges. And I remember them [being] kind of multi-colored, kind of pastel as opposed to primary colors. I don't remember them moving—kind of like moving, but just hovering each in place . . . they definitely appeared solid. Their edges and lights and colors were just diffused, almost like a fog around them or something."

Kim, although only five years old at the time, also remembers the incident, though perhaps not in as much detail. She does remember seeing at least one metallic disk hovering and glaring brightly in the sunlight. "We looked over on the mountain there, and on top of the mountain was a flying saucer. And it was silver and just hovering over this mountain. We all got out and looked at it. We were like, 'Wow, look at this flying saucer!' No fear. No fear at all. We were just totally amazed. We just stood there, got out of the car, stopped, stood there, and looked at it . . . it seemed close. It didn't seem high in the sky and far away. It seemed close enough to see the details that it was a silver-disk type thing . . . it was like the old-type disk, silvery, round, is what I remember."

All three witnesses agree that the disks were very large, larger than their own Volkswagon bus. None of them were the least bit frightened. In fact, both Lisa and Kim found the event very exciting.

After about fifteen minutes, the disks began to move. As Beverly remembered, "They just kind of came together and I can't say that they landed. They just kind of settled there. And all of a sudden they just came apart and went off separate ways. One went one way and the other went the other way."

It was at this point that Beverly decided to take some action. She gathered the kids and rushed them back into the van. She had only one thought on her mind: get home and get the binoculars and camera.

It was at this point that something very mysterious occurred. All three witnesses simultaneously experienced a period of missing time. As Beverly related, "It was so strange because I said, 'Well, let's run home. Let's get in the bus and get home real quick and get the binoculars and look at them real good, see what's going on.' So what was so strange was that we got in the bus, I guess, came home, but none of us remember coming home, and we didn't think about it until the next day. I don't know what time we got home or anything, so it was really strange. So I just said, 'Oh, we won't say anything about this because everybody will think we're crazy.'"

Unknown to Beverly at the time, thousands, perhaps millions of people across the world have experienced missing time in conjunction with a UFO encounter. Many of these people have undergone regressive hypnosis and recalled the period of amnesia. In nearly every missing time case, the witnesses remember being onboard the UFO.

Back in 1961, however, missing time abductions were just beginning to appear. Beverly, of course, had never heard of them and therefore had no way of knowing what had happened to her and her children.

She is adamant that her memory of the event is clear except for the segment of missing time. She clearly remembers getting into the bus. However, she doesn't remember driving home or arriving home. It wasn't until the next morning that she even remembered the UFO sighting and her original plan to get the binoculars. Only then did she realize that there was time missing. The first thing she did was speak to the girls and ask them if they remembered the encounter. Both of them did.

Kim clearly remembered the odd experience of missing time. "We were going to get a camera and binoculars and come back to look at it, but we forgot about it until the next day. And when we went home, we didn't remember. It was broad daylight, and then that was it."

Lisa's memory of the missing time event matches very closely with her mother's. "I just remember standing there and looking at them. And as I was looking at them, my mom's saying, 'Let's go get the binoculars.' I remember feeling like I didn't want to leave. You know how you feel like you might miss something if you leave? I don't remember getting into the car."

Although Lisa doesn't remember getting into the car, she does remember a detail that neither her sister nor her mother recalled. "We went home to get the binoculars, but we didn't remember to get the binoculars. I remember somebody saying we had been gone an awful long time just to go to the store. And we couldn't figure out why. Nobody remembered about the binoculars until the next day. We didn't remember why we had gone home. I just remember somebody saying we had been gone two or three hours . . . I wouldn't say I remember coming home. I remember being home. I would put it that way. Do I remember the drive home? No. I remember the drive down the hill, standing at that place and looking at these three objects . . . it seemed to me there was a fight about how long we were gone, between my parents."

It is highly unlikely that three excited witnesses would suddenly forget they were seeing UFOs. However, memory loss in conjunction with a close encounter is a red flag to the UFO investigator indicating that the encounter is more extensive than a mere sighting. In fact, Budd Hopkins titled his first book *Missing Time* simply because it was such a consistent feature of UFO abductions.

Were Beverly Smith and her two children abducted? None of them have undergone hypnosis to recover their memories, nor do they have plans to do so. They all agree that their encounter may be more extensive than they can consciously recall and someday, they may try to find out what happened.

But whatever occurred to them, they were left with a good feeling. They did not want to dig up any traumatic memories thirty years after the event. As far as they're concerned, it's the past. As Lisa said, "For a time I was interested in having maybe regressive hypnosis or something to see if anything happened to me, but since I didn't have any recurring dreams or apparent losses of time except for that time, I just really decided that it wasn't worth going into, mostly because I have a sense of well-being and a good feeling about it . . . and since it feels that way, and since the reading I've done [indicates] that some people have pretty traumatic experiences and that sense of well-being is put there to protect you, I think I'd like to leave it that way."

Beverly never told anybody except her family and friends. Her children had the same reaction. As Kim said, "It's not something I've told anybody about because nobody believes you. It's not something you go around and brag about. It was just something that we all saw that I'll never forget."

The Smiths' encounter took over thirty years to be reported in any official capacity. It was only through a series of coincidences that it ever came to be included in this book. It is highly likely that there are many other families just like the Smiths and the Martins who have experienced extensive UFO encounters, but have told nobody for fear of ridicule. In fact, many UFO researchers agree that perhaps as many as one in fifty people have experienced an onboard UFO encounter.

In a UFO wave area, that percentage is probably much higher.

8

Mysterious Lights
at Night

THE MOST COMMON type of
UFO sighting is unexplained lights in the night sky.
Because Topanga is a UFO flap area, I have uncovered
many of these kinds of reports. Although such reports
are common, they are no less interesting.

Kim Smith, who experienced a missing-time UFO
encounter with her mother and sister on Grandview
Drive in the early 'sixties, had yet another encounter with
a UFO over Topanga. The incident took place in 1974,
down Old Canyon Road, near Callicamp Campgrounds.

It was late at night and Kim and a friend were laying outside watching the stars. It was a warm, clear
night, well past midnight. They had been watching the
stars for hours and dawn was quickly approaching. It
was then that Kim saw something totally unexpected.

What at first appeared to be a very bright star suddenly began to move. The star-like object had been in
the sky for hours and had not moved in the slightest.
But when the sky began to brighten, the star-like

object began to move. Kim knew instantly that it was not a star.

"I sat up on the mountaintop, and I'd been up there most of the night looking out at the stars, looking over the basin. And when dawn came, this light that looked like a star just ze'ed back and forth at really fast speeds and just took off out of the atmosphere. This thing, it just took off and zipped back and forth . . . I watched it take off. I mean, it wasn't a shooting star. It moved in straight lines, but only like a zigzag. Definitely a straight line, really fast speed, and then out . . . it wasn't anything I've ever seen."

Although the sighting lasted only seconds, it was long enough for Kim to get a good look at the object. "It was pretty big. It wasn't like a little star. It was a pretty big, bright light—a planet-looking thing. I was watching all the stars and this one looked really strong, like a planet or star . . . ."

When it zigzagged straight out of the atmosphere, Kim knew that it was no shooting star. Shooting stars do not zigzag, nor do they travel upwards. It was much too fast to be a satellite, airplane, helicopter, or any conventional aircraft. And the weather conditions excluded the possibility of ball-lightning.

Just because the sighting is a mysterious light, doesn't make it any less significant. In fact, this type of sighting is often just as difficult to explain as many sightings of metallic disks. Kim believes that what she saw was an actual spaceship. However, she has learned that trying to convince people that she's telling the truth is not worth the trouble. "That's another thing I just don't tell people about . . . I saw it and it was unusual. As far as I'm concerned, it was a spaceship."

A few months after the June 14, 1992 sightings, I put up several flyers throughout Topanga, asking if anybody else had seen UFOs. I figured if Topanga was truly experiencing a UFO wave, then I should receive some type of response from the flyer. There had to be many witnesses who hadn't yet told their stories.

Almost immediately, I began getting calls.

Johnny has lived in Topanga for over twenty years, and is well-known in the community. When he saw my UFO flyer pinned to the bulletin board at the local market, he copied down the number and gave me a call. He was relieved to finally find someone who would actually listen to what he had to say.

Johnny reports that he has seen UFOs over Topanga on more than one occasion. One summer night in 1973 or 1974, when Johnny was still in high school, he and two friends drove up Santa Maria Road and pulled off to watch the sky. It was a clear night with a full moon.

Suddenly, Johnny and his friends noticed some strange lights darting low in the sky towards the south. Johnny guessed that the lights were hovering over the Entrada area and Topanga State Park.

Most UFO sightings are relatively brief. Johnny and his friends, however, remember watching the strange lights hovering and darting for hours on end. "I and some high school friends . . . saw some lights off in the distance, over the distant hills, that were doing things that planes don't do, turning at right angles and just making weird right angle turns. And I don't think a helicopter could have done it either. It just seemed a little odd. But it was kind of far away so it was really hard to tell exactly what was going on."

Johnny estimated that the lights were about two or three miles away. Except for their strange darting movements, the lights looked very much like stars. However, there was another strange detail: the lights would appear and disappear at random. "There wasn't anything there and then they would just appear . . . there were lights that would just appear above the horizon. And the skyline was real distinct, so I don't believe I was seeing a helicopter coming up behind a mountain because it was pretty clear where the horizon, the mountain-line was. And some of these lights would just sort of go off and on, go at right angles and things like that."

Eventually, either the lights went away or Johnny and his friends left. He doesn't quite recall. However, he does remember seeing similar lights on other occasions. "I've seen other lights like that at other times up in the mountains here . . . that's the type of thing I've seen quite a bit. But they're always so far away and it's kind of hard to say what's going on . . . although there have been a couple of instances when I've seen lights that were not on the horizon but were directly over-head, that covered the sky within five, even two or three seconds, one of them as I recall was really, really quick."

Johnny is certain they were not satellites or shooting stars. "I don't believe they were satellites. It seems to me one of them made a turn so it couldn't have been a satellite, not a ninety-degree turn or anything, but it made a turn . . . the shooting stars I've seen have always been kind of short. You see them and then they disappear. I have seen some longer shooting stars. I remember when I was a kid, I saw a light that went across two thirds of the sky, and it was much, much thinner than you would think a shooting star would be. It went down below the horizon so it didn't appear like a shooting star at all."

Unfortunately, Johnny has never seen any UFOs close-up. However, because he has seen UFOs over Topanga so often, he is convinced the canyon is definitely a UFO hotspot.

Another person who answered my flyer is Topanga resident Ethan Holtzman. His first words to me were: "I just saw a UFO!" Ethan went on to explain how he had recently seen a large object that appeared to be landing in the creek along Topanga Canyon Boulevard. A few days later, he saw my flyer and gave me a call.

His encounter began around midnight on September 22, 1992. Ethan was driving north on the boulevard, about one mile south of Old Topanga Canyon Road. He reached a spot along the road where a fatal motorcycle accident had occurred years previous. He was suddenly overcome by a strange sense of déjà vu regarding the accident. At that point, something strange happened. A large fiery-red object appeared and began to land in the exact spot where the motorcycle accident had occurred.

As Ethan recalled, "I was driving . . . right by the video store, I went around the corner and I was having déjà vu. And then I came on the straightaway, and right up there on the left was where two people died on a motorcycle not too long ago. And I saw the bodies there. And right there, I was having a big flashback or something, like I'd seen it all before. And then I looked up and there was this huge, red ball of fire, and it looked like it just fell. And it wasn't a shooting star; it was like five-hundred times the size of that. I don't know if it was a fireball, but it was red and it just fell straight down and disappeared. And I just stopped. It was really weird because I was feeling so strange just before I saw it. I don't know what it was . . . I saw a solid mass. I saw it. It fell. It just fell out of the sky. And it looked like about the size of the sun. It was a deep red. I didn't hear any noise."

Ethan does not insist that he saw an actual alien spaceship. He is only reporting what he saw. He admits that the experience was actually terrifying. And he also says that he was not the only witness. As he said, "Maybe it was a fireball. I'm not sure. Or maybe it was Army testing, but it was just really out of the ordinary . . . I saw a Hispanic guy running the opposite direction after it. I didn't stop though because I was freaked out, because I thought the aliens were abducting me."

Unfortunately, Ethan was unable to indentify the other witness, who was apparently a vagrant, and all attempts to locate him failed. Still, Ethan found it comforting to have someone else confirm his sighting.

Did Ethan and the Hispanic man see a fireball? Technically speaking, a fireball is simply a large, bright meteor or shooting star. Of course, it's possible they both saw a close-up shooting star. However, Ethan is very clear that the object was a solid mass that fell straight down. Fireballs are seen high up and are visible high up in the atmosphere for miles around. This doesn't match what Ethan saw.

And there's also the déjà vu connection. This is perhaps the most mysterious aspect of Ethan's encounter. Was he in an altered state of consciousness which allowed him to hallucinate a UFO? This is highly doubtful as there was another witness. Ethan himself doesn't understand the connection.

But as we have seen, there are some Topanga cases involving apparent telepathic communication and the answer may lie in that direction. I would later uncover other reports involve telepathic communication with UFOs.

These three reports are very different, but they all point to one fact: there is something about Topanga that is conducive to UFOs. And the fact the there was such a quick response to the flyers indicates that there are probably many other residents who have seen the objects but don't know who to call.

I continued to receive calls from the flyers. Some were from witnesses who were willing to share their stories but didn't want to be recorded or formally interviewed. Others had friends who had seen UFOs over Topanga. Some were just interested in how the investigation was going.

The calls from the flyers came in pretty regularly. Whenever they stopped, I would go check on the flyers and invariably, they would be removed. As soon as I would replace them, I would begin to get calls again. However, soon after I put new flyers up, they are usually removed within days or weeks, presumably by interested residents.

Still, I continued to put up the flyers. Later on, I would get more responses and more incredible reports.

9

A Bedroom Visitation

FOR A PLACE to qualify as a UFO flap area, the full range of encounters must be represented. While mysterious lights are the most common type of report, a close-up encounter with an alien entity is perhaps the least common. These types of encounters are also highly controversial, and for that reason, few people are willing to brave the ridicule and disbelief that often results from coming forward to tell their stories.

People who experience alien entity visitations usually tell only family and close friends. The last thing they want to do is tell the world that not only do they believe aliens exist, but also that they have been visited by them.

However skeptical people may be of such reports, it is a fact that in a UFO flap area, during a wave of sightings, the number of abductions and face-to-face encounters is disproportionately large. In other words, living in a UFO flap area dramatically increases your chances of not only seeing a UFO, but experiencing a close encounter of the third kind.

Just this event happened to one resident who lives in the Entrada area, near Topanga State Park.

Susan, who saw the star-like UFO in Topanga State Park on July 14 with three friends, is the central witness in this case. Susan has lived in Topanga with her husband, Jonathon, and their two sons for over twenty-five years. She chose Topanga because it was a close-knit rural community near a large city, the perfect place to raise their children. At the time, she had no idea that they had moved into a UFO flap area.

Susan was neither a UFO skeptic nor a believer. She had never thought much about UFOs simply because the subject had never really come up. So when she had her experience, she had no idea how to interpret it.

It occurred during the first week of January, 1991, over one year prior to her first UFO sighting. She had gone to bed one evening, sleeping alone to avoid being awakened by her husband's snoring. Sometime very early in the morning, she experienced what is known as a "bedroom visitation." This term is used to described a particular type of UFO encounter in which entities enter directly into a person's bedroom.

The ordeal began when Susan awoke to sense a presence in the room. She quickly discovered that she was also unable to move. Susan has a remarkable mind for details, so I'll allow her to explain her experience in her own words:

"This is what I recall. On this early morning I was having a very intense dream. I don't believe it was a dream; I call it that as my first line of defense. I'd say that I had some kind of an experience. I remember that I was overwhelmed with paralysis. I was lying on my stomach. I was facing out from the bed and facing my bookshelf where I have notepaper and writing material. And it was dark. I don't have an idea of the time because there is a clock in the room but it's at the other side of the bed, away from me.

"And I lay there paralyzed, consumed with fear because I sensed that there was someone else in the room. And I was so fearful or so paralyzed that I could not move. My head was on a pillow to the side, and there was a presence of this figure at the foot of the bed. And I sensed that it was small. I sensed that it was maybe about three or four feet tall. And I, as a tall woman, would know if the figure or the energy field was higher.

"I never felt that it was something I could see. I sensed that it was something that I truly felt. And I remember I sensed that it was like a column or cylinder in that there was energy emanating from it, or the energy was rotating, or somehow there was movement of energy. And then this energy came close to my head. It moved from the foot of the bed to my head. And I sensed that a strand of my hair was picked up and was cut. And then the energy moved back to the foot of the bed.

"I had blankets over me. It was a January evening; it was cool. The next thing I felt was that there was something penetrating my vagina. And it was as if this pen that I hold in my hand was merely inserted and then removed. And I could not move. I could not scream. I could not express anything. I lay there simply in fear.

"And it was another couple of moments, again I have no sense of time, but I felt that after a short period of time, the energy simply disappeared. It was gone. I heard nothing that night. I don't remember animals, dogs, coyotes, owls, or other kinds of birds. I heard nothing, but that's not unusual because sometimes there are periods of silence when we don't hear animals at all.

"It took me a very, very long time to move my body from the position I was in. And I say that only because as I was beginning finally to move; I was quite stiff because I had laid there with such tension for a long period of time. As I was coming out of this paralysis, out of what I felt was almost a state of hypnosis because not only was my body paralyzed, but my mind . . . it was like I was coming up, like I was drugged.

"I've had medication for surgery in the past and I know what it's like to come out of a very deep sleep where you are fighting for consciousness, for brightness, for alertness. And as I was coming out of this deep state, I remember being chilled like I was breaking out in a sweat. And I was trembling because I didn't know what I had experienced, and my physical reaction was unlike anything I have ever experienced in a dream state before. I have vivid dreams. I remember some of them. I try, when I wake up in the middle of the night, to write some of them down or make notations or drawings so that I can remember. I have never felt anything that was as intense as this. I tend not to have nightmares, although I certainly would say that I've had my share of fear of the unknown. But I've never had a series of ongoing nightmares where my life or the lives of any members of my family have been threatened by any kind of thing.

"And so when I was finally able to put together my composure and move my body and get up out of bed, I could hear out in the kitchen, my husband and son beginning to make breakfast. And I threw on a bathrobe and came on out and just sort of stumbled into my husband's arms and I said, 'I just want you to hold me. I have had the most terrible dream I have ever experienced in my life. I am so shocked by it, I can't even talk about it right now. Maybe I can a little bit later in the day, but I want you to know that I have been so upset by my dream that please understand if I'm a little bit out of sorts and that I need to be alone.'

"So they understood and they proceeded with their activities. And for the rest of the day I just sort of mumbled and fumbled around and tried to do things that had to be done. Being self-employed and [sometimes] unemployed, I don't always have a schedule that I have to keep. So I was able to take the time, I had the freedom to try to put it in perspective. And I didn't talk about it for three days because it was so strong, it was so predominant.

"I didn't have any problem sleeping for the next couple of nights, but I simply didn't want to talk about it. On about the third day, I sat my husband down and said, 'This is what happened to me. This is the dream that I had. And I want you to understand because it was so powerful that I may have something like this happen again, and I want you to understand what happened to me the first time. So if I have another dream like this, you'll understand what I've gone through.'

"So I shared the story with him and he didn't make anything out of it, and I didn't other than what I've described. It was a long time before I began to think that there might be more to it than it being a dream."

About a month later, Susan and her husband were invited to stay with some friends in Northern California. However, when the time came to leave, the friends called and canceled. One of the friends just happened to be a well-known UFO researcher. Susan had met him briefly a few years earlier and, in fact, was given an audiotape of one of his lectures. Susan was interested in hearing what was on the tape, but simply never found the time.

So when she found out that the trip was canceled, she called up her friend and said, "Oh, I am so disappointed because I would really like to meet and talk with him. I had a dream that was very perplexing to me and I don't know what it might mean, but he might be able to help me understand."

Susan surprised herself by her request. "Why I said that I have no idea because I hadn't yet listened to the tape. I had, I must tell you, no knowledge of UFO/ET experience or phenomena. I only knew of my personal situation. I had never read science-fiction growing up. I didn't watch *Star Trek*. I had none of the so-called popular responses to this kind of curiosity."

When the UFO researcher heard about Susan's dream, he expressed his desire that Susan and her husband, Jonathon, visit anyway. He felt that it was important Susan speak with him. After consulting with him, Susan decided to be hypnotized to recall her experience.

As she says, "We talked, he and I, about what occurred. He put me under hypnosis. And I must tell you that I somehow blanked out some of the things that he said after the first hypnotic session. I think that from his perspective, what happened to me as it might relate to extraterrestrial intelligence or other beings was not conclusive.

"I remember what had occurred so vividly that I really didn't need to be hypnotized, but he nevertheless wanted to probe for further information. I think he, professionally as a researcher, did not want to say conclusively that I had had a contact. But what he was trying to do was allay my fears because I was very shaken by the experience. And this is what led me to believe that he had a pretty specific or definitive belief that I had had some kind of experience that was other than a dream, because he said, 'You know, ETs are not wanting to hurt people.' He said, 'Stop and think that there might have been reasons, positive reasons, for what happened to you.'

"I mean, for me, that was a dead giveaway. He didn't have to say to me, 'Well, yes, you did have some kind of visitation.' But when he couched it in those terms, it was like, 'All right, yes.' The kind of sexual probing that occurred—that could have had as much a positive bene-fit as negative. I didn't feel physically harmed by the experience. It was a violation of my psyche, my body. I did not give anyone permission to do that. But I had to look at it and say, 'Yes, maybe he's correct. Maybe there was, will be, or is a positive benefit. Unknown to me, but maybe there is a positive side to that.'

"So I accepted that and it made me feel much better because it made me think, 'All right, I'm not doing myself any good by continuing to harbor this type of fear because I'm reacting truly emotionally without any other basis than just my own recall of the experience.'"

Over the next few months, Susan had a total of three hypnotic regressions. No new details of her experience were uncovered, though there were some indications that Susan may have had other experiences at a different time. Under hypnosis, the UFO researcher asked her about other possible experiences, and she recalled being in a cave. Later she had a dream of the same cave when suddenly, the walls became smooth and shiny and she could see a strange table in the center of the room. These details are typically described by abductees. Susan, however, elected to stop exploring these memories for the time-being.

One of the results of her experience was an intense interest in the subject of UFOs. Susan began reading books, attending seminars, and connecting with other UFO researchers. The experience also affected her in other ways.

"I have become very much involved in the environmental field . . . I don't know if this is tied into my own ET experience, which I now believe actually occurred; I don't think it was a dream. I think it was an experience that I had in real time. I've had two visions that came as dreams. The first being to save seeds, plant seeds. So I've been doing that off all the foods that I eat.

"I've also become almost a total vegetarian, although I've been leaning in that direction . . . for years. But of all the fresh fruits particularly that I eat, I will save the seeds—of grapes, berries, peaches, plums. Anyway, my family thinks I'm a bit nuts, but that's okay. I collect their seeds too. 'Don't throw away your grape seeds please! I'll take them!'

"And the second vision I had was to grow beans. I'm going to become a bean farmer before this life is over . . . and I don't think that those two visions are unrelated to the dream experience that I had. I think that they're somehow tied in."

While Susan's husband remains skeptical of UFOs, Susan also feels that she may have had another experience. She also feels that her sons may be involved. She explained, "I don't think the story is finished . . . there may be certain conclusions drawn midway through the experience which may not end for a very, very long time, and I'd rather have any kind of conclusions drawn when I feel that it's appropriate to do so . . . It's interesting that even someone like my husband doesn't feel as if I've had any kind of extraterrestrial/UFO kind of experience. He comes from his own set of beliefs and experiences. So I'm dealing, even on the home-front, with issues that I'd just assume not to have to deal with. But we live with them. And you certainly know my children . . . I have a feeling that both boys have had contact of one kind or another and we are in the process of getting to explore that."

Susan obviously feels that her experience is related to UFOs and I agree, or her account would not have been included in this book. Although Susan never actually saw aliens, her experience corroborates with the experiences of many others.

There is a phenomenon known as "night terror" in which a person becomes lucid during the dream state, when the body is naturally paralyzed by a brain mechanism that prevents injuries from occurring by physically acting out the dream.

Did Susan simply experience "night terror?"

I do not believe that the dream explanation is sufficient for several reasons. First, her account matches up very closely with other accounts in which people have seen aliens. One detail that many witnesses report is that the aliens are very short. Susan estimated three or four feet tall. Many other witnesses report samples being taken of skin, hair, nails, and even reproductive material. This is certainly true in Susan's case.

Also, Susan's reactions to the experience are not consistent with a dream. She was physically affected by the experience, even after it was over. As she said, it was like being drugged. Not only was it one of the scariest experiences of her life, it caused a transformation in her personality. She became intensely interested in subjects that before interested her only slightly.

Further indications of the reality of her experience are the other snippets she has remembered of being inside a room that is the exact description of the inside of a UFO, and the experience occurred in the center of the busiest part of a UFO flap area.

Ultimately, however, Susan's experience remains a mystery. However, as she said, the story may not be over. Certainly for other people in Topanga Canyon, it was only the beginning.

10

When You Wish Upon a UFO

WHEN I FIRST realized that Topanga Canyon was a UFO flap area, I did what anyone would do who has lived there most of his life. I began examining my own past for any memories of a possible UFO encounter. Although I've spent many nights outside in Topanga, I had no memories of seeing a UFO. I once saw a fireball arc across the sky, leaving a purple trail that lasted ten minutes. One year during the Perseid meteor showers, my brother and I observed over seventy shootings stars in one hour.

However, after the June 14, 1992 sightings, my awareness of UFOs over Topanga was considerably heightened. I discovered that most investigators of UFO flap areas end up seeing UFOs themselves. Although the reports flooded in, I, however, wasn't seeing anything. During the summer activity, I spent several nights camped out in the areas where the objects were being reported. Not once did I see anything.

Because my family lives in Topanga, I asked each of them to keep their eyes out for strange objects in the sky. I knew that many other families in Topanga were experiencing encounters, and since so many of my family members lived there too, it seemed only logical that sooner or later, one of them would have an encounter.

To my surprise, it turned out that way.

My oldest brother was the first to admit he had seen UFOs over Topanga. He was with two friends up on the Saddlepeak area when they saw bright lights in the sky above them. At first my brother thought that it was old artillery being exploded over the coast. He called the Point Mugu Military Base, which denied the activity. He did not report the incident as a UFO, saying instead that the lights were probably flares.

However, I spoke with the friends who were with him that night, and they said the lights were not flares. They moved at right angles very quickly, all across the sky. I told my brother this, and he said that the movement was not at right angles, but rather slowly downward, at which point the lights would fade—all of which is consistent with flares. My brother is somewhat skeptical of the UFO phenomenon. Nevertheless, on another occasion, during the summer of 1992, he walked through Topanga State Park, where he saw a star-like object zip quickly across the sky—too fast for a plane, too slow for a shooting star. He told me the story with a quizzical smile, not quite ready to admit that he actually saw an unidentified flying object.

The next report came from another brother and his wife. While driving northward along Topanga Boulevard, about two miles south of Old Topanga Canyon Road, they saw a bright blue light fall slowly downward. They said it was much too bright and slow to be a shooting star, and that it moved straight down in the area of Old Topanga Canyon. Although the sighting may not seem dramatic, it had the earmarks investigators look for, including strange appearances and strange movements.

Finally, yet another brother and sister-in-law were inside their Topanga Canyon home when they saw strange flashes of light coming from outside their front window. Despite my recent ranting that a UFO wave was in progress, none of them wanted to get up and stop the video they were watching. So they just ignored the flashes. My brother, however, reports that the flashes were definitely not headlights, and that he doesn't understand what could have caused them. Of course, I chastised them for not going out to at least check.

Then, one mid-August evening in 1992, at around 9:00 P.M., I headed south on Topanga Canyon Boulevard when I saw a bright white light hovering over Topanga State Park, near Entrada. At first I wasn't really impressed. Although the light was definitely hovering in place, and was at least ten times the brightness of a star, and low on the horizon, I knew that it could easily be a plane that was heading in my direction. I had seen this effect of a hovering light many times. Each time, the light would eventually "wink out" and the lights of the plane would become visible. I knew that the effect was caused by the plane turning. The extremely bright landing lights only appeared to wink out because they were no longer facing me.

So I simply assumed I was seeing a plane and waited for it to turn and make its wing lights visible. Sure enough, the bright light suddenly winked out. But to my utter surprise, there was nothing there. There were no other lights, no plane. The night was clear and I could easily see that there were not only no wing lights, but no plane. There was nothing at all where there had seconds ago been an extremely bright white light.

I recall thinking, "I saw that!" I knew it was unusual, but I didn't stop the car. I just kept driving.

That was my first Topanga sighting. Others were soon to follow. On one occasion in mid-summer 1994, I was at my brother's house along Cheney Drive. It was around 10:00 P.M. when I had the impulse to go outside and look at the sky. I went into the backyard and to my surprise, instantly saw what looked like a shooting star flit downward. I marveled at the coincidence and then told myself that that's all it was—a coincidence. And then, at that exact moment, I saw another apparent shooting star in the exact same place. At that point, I could only wonder. UFOs calling me mentally outside to look at them? Hey, hadn't other people reported the same thing? What would be next?

My next sighting occurred a few months later. It was early evening and I was at a friend's house on Saddlepeak, looking eastward over the canyon ridge, when I saw a bright flash of light turn on and off. It was above the ridge and much too bright to be a car or anything from the ground. It was totally silent and gone in a split second. I was stunned and wondered if anybody else saw it when someone at the house shouted, "What was that light?"

We discussed what we saw but were unable to come up with an explanation. This didn't seem to bother my friend, but it did bother me. I was seeing the Topanga UFOs regularly and I still didn't know what was going on.

By now I realized that what was happening to other families in Topanga was also happening to my own. Some of my family members were seeing the objects, and some weren't. Those that saw them believed in them, those that didn't, didn't.

On March 7, 1993, my sister Valerie experienced a very interesting encounter in Topanga. At the time, she lived high on the ridge along Observation Drive, only a few hundred yards away from where Beverly Smith and her two daughters had a missing-time encounter in the early 'sixties.

On that evening, Valerie was busy with her new baby, who was less than a week old. Her boyfriend, the baby's father, lived with her and helped to take care of her and the new baby.

At around 9:30 P.M. they went to sleep. Because of the new baby, Valerie had been having trouble sleeping. As she lay there in bed, she noticed what looked like a very bright star low on the eastern horizon.

She did what she often does upon seeing a star for the first time in the evening. She made a wish. "I was laying in bed, looking out the window and I saw a bright star out of the crack of where the curtains come together. And I wished on the star, like I do sometimes. It was the first star I saw that night . . . it just looked like a star. It didn't move."

Every few hours Valerie had to get up and feed the baby. Throughout the night, she noticed that the star was still in the exact same position, but really didn't think anything about it.

The very next night, after they went to bed, the star was there again. Valerie made another wish, but this time, something extraordinary happened. The "star" did something stars cannot do. ". . . right after I wished on the star again, the light went out . . . no, wait a second. That's not right. The star started moving up and down the crack of where the curtains come together. Up and down, real slow, in a straight line. And then it started moving sideways, horizontally, in a straight line . . . then it went back to the crack and the light went out, and a little red light came on and a little blue light came on a little bit below it and to the right. And that light—these two lights—were moving sideways across the sky."

Valerie stared at the lights, puzzled. They didn't look or move like any aircraft she'd ever seen, though there was no doubt that it was an aircraft of some kind. The object moved across the horizon, horizontally and vertically, at least twenty times all night long.

As Valerie watched the object, she began to get the distinct impression that it was watching her. "It went pretty much all night until I fell asleep, about 3:30 A.M. I was with the baby, and plus, it was making me kind of nervous. I thought that it might be watching me. It made me nervous. And then I went to the window and opened it up and looked outside, thinking it might have been a reflection of something in the window of the mirror behind me, but I opened the door and looked outside and it was definitely out there."

When Valerie opened the door, she scanned the entire sky. To her surprise, she saw two other identical objects in the sky, one hovering towards the north, the other toward the south. She was unable to see towards the west because the room faced only east. The other objects were moving in the same way as the first one. "I didn't notice them at first, but after I opened the door and looked out, I saw a couple [of them]. I saw another one in the [opposite] side of the sky, and then one over on the other side. So the first one I saw was in the middle. I didn't look behind the house. There might have been more."

Valerie had absolutely no idea what the objects could be. "They were red and blue lights. The red light was a little above the blue light. The blue light was on the bottom . . . it didn't look like a helicopter or an airplane. And it didn't move like a helicopter or an airplane. It went sideways and up and down. It didn't fly around. It was only in two places. The other two were going sideways. The other two didn't go up and down. They never came together . . . that's why I didn't think it was an airplane. And plus it moved back and forth in the same place. An airplane wouldn't do that. An airplane would go, and then go away."

If Valerie thought things were strange at this point, they were about to get much stranger. Around 11:00 P.M. she noticed another bizarre detail—though she lived in a relatively populated section of Topanga, no lights shone from the surrounding houses. "I did look out the window at the other houses, and all the other lights were out in every other house, every other house . . . the one across the way . . . usually there are other lights on. I guess everybody was out of town or something, I don't know."

As it got later, Valerie became more nervous. The feeling that she was being watched grew so strong that she decided to awaken her boyfriend. But to her surprise, he wouldn't wake up. "I tried to wake him up because I got nervous. I thought it was watching me. But he wouldn't wake up . . . that was about two o'clock in the morning. I watched it a while longer after that. It stayed there sometimes, and then it moved sometimes. But it really did make me nervous because I thought it was watching . . . I thought that maybe it was going to come down and take me away, or my baby or something, because I just had [the] baby . . . five days before that. It sure did make me nervous. I mean, I started getting really nervous. It was kind of weird." When her boyfriend wouldn't wake up, Valerie briefly thought of calling me. She knew of my interest in UFOs, but, as she says, "I didn't want to sound like a scared lady."

Valerie already felt foolish enough for trying to wake her boyfriend so he could protect her from the objects. "I also felt kind of weird about waking him up and telling him, 'There's a UFO outside!' But I did. I tried to wake him and say, 'I think there's a UFO out there,' but he wouldn't wake up. I didn't think he would believe me." Unknown to Valerie, this detail of being literally unable to wake up somebody is yet another indicator of an extensive UFO encounter.

If the object had simply left, Valerie would have been fine. It was only because it wouldn't go away that she felt any fear. "That was weird. That was one of the reasons it scared me. It kept going back and forth, and you know, it made me nervous."

An interesting aspect of Valerie's sighting was her feeling of being observed. She is not the first Topanga UFO witness to report this feeling. She felt that the object was not only aware of her presence, but that it knew she was watching it. "The one I saw first was the one in the middle, the one that was between the crack of the curtains. That was another reason I thought it was watching me. It was right in-between the curtains. It was freaky."

Did Valerie see alien spaceships?

Of course, it's virtually impossible to prove that she did. However, Valerie used to be extremely skeptical of UFOs. Now she is not as skeptical as she used to be.

The most ironic aspect of her encounter is that she thought she was wishing upon a star when, evidently, she was wishing upon a UFO. Normally we don't expect stars to suddenly move, wink out, and turn different colors after we wish upon them. This apparent communication deeply impressed Valerie. "It shocked me because it was a bright, white light first, and then the white light went out and instantly the red light came on and a little blue light."

Did the object actually respond to Valerie's wish? "I don't know. I was looking at it. It was right after I wished on it because I thought it was a star . . . like 'Star light, star bright, first star I've seen tonight, I wish I may, I wish I might, have the wish I wish tonight.' Well, I didn't wish for a UFO!"

Valerie does not remember experiencing any missing time. She doesn't remember any unusual animal sounds. She had no dreams that she would associate with UFOs. Nor has she noticed any mysterious scars on her body.

Later, on October 18, 1993, Valerie saw another object swoop low through the canyon. It was perfectly silent and moved quickly away to the south.

All these encounters in my own family literally hit home. We were living in a UFO hotspot and some of us were having encounters. Of course, the subject has caused a minor split in the family. Those who haven't seen the objects continue to remain skeptical. Again, the pattern is quite clear.

It also became clear to me that what was happening to my family was, in fact, happening to many other families throughout Topanga. Although not talked about, the UFO encounters were having a profound effect on everyone.

Witnesses often said they did not tell their families about their encounters for fear of disbelief. Others spoke candidly with their families and found out the hard way how skeptical people can be. And yet, other families have been brought closer together by their experiences.

For many Topanga Canyon residents, living in a UFO hotspot definitely has been a challenge.

11

A Helicopter UFO Chase

As the sightings and encounters continued, I alerted the local UFO groups that Topanga was a hotspot. I also began lecturing about the incidents in attempt to get the word out.

However, one of the obvious indications of a UFO flap area is the constant reports of UFO activity. For whatever reason, the objects are drawn to the area and simply will not go away. The autumn of 1993 produced more solid reports of sightings. The wave was still in progress.

In mid-September that year, an encounter occurred which betrayed just how complex the Topanga Canyon UFO encounters really are.

The central witness to this sighting is Dr. David Phillips who is a professor and head of the History Department at Santa Monica College, and Topanga resident. His case was referred to me by a fellow UFO investigator after he heard that the encounter took place in Topanga Canyon.

Dr. Phillips has lived in the area for many years, at an approximate altitude of 1,500 feet on Fernwood, but has never had an experience like the one he had on that particular fall evening. It all began when he was awakened out of a peaceful sleep. As he recalled, "It was about two-thirty in the morning and I was awakened by the sound of helicopters, very low. And I got up, looked around and thought, 'What the hell are helicopters doing out at this time?' Rarely do I hear them that low in Topanga. I went to the back of my house which faces east, and I looked towards Topanga State Park. I can see real clearly around Eagle Rock, up there. And I could see three helicopters. One was stationary, perhaps a thousand feet in the air, or two thousand. And the other two were real low, moving under it, scanning for something. And they moved up and about and around, and they were there for maybe—I watched them for ten minutes.

"There wasn't any other activity around. And then, towards Topanga Boulevard, in that direction which is kind of a southwest direction, I could see what appeared to be the headlights of a vehicle, and they were really zooming down the road. And even at this distance you could see that they were really hauling over that road which I've hiked many times. . . .

"I sort of watched with great curiosity. I sort of thought, 'Well, it's the sheriff or somebody's after the bad guys in the park.' I couldn't figure out what it was though.

"I was standing there watching it. Then, from left to right, going down right over Topanga creek where the boulevard is, going down the canyon towards the ocean, this craft just went by in my field of vision. It probably lasted one or two seconds. That's all it took to go from left to right. And it was just as clear as a bell. It was very light. And the helicopters were behind it. And this thing just scooted down the canyon, silently. I couldn't see any lights on it. It was just bright. It was silvery and light . . . it was kind of disk-shaped with sort of a little bubble on top. Bubble's the wrong word, but a little level on top. And it just transferred very quickly. It was very clear. And it was absolutely silent. It just went down the creek over the highway, with the hill in the background."

The location of Dr. Phillips' sighting is significant because other witnesses have noticed a great deal of activity in the same area. Said Dr. Phillips, "They were right over the State Park because I could see their searchlights going down on the State Park. I have a clear view of the State Park from the back of my house, which is all glass. And I can just stand there and look at the State Park. And I could see helicopters obviously looking for something. The two events may not be connected. It may be that they were sheriff's helicopters looking for some bad person. Or they may be related. I just don't have a clue."

Dr. Phillips was unable to tell what kind of vehicles were racing down the road, however, this itself is highly unusual. The road is actually a dirt firebreak and is closed to public traffic. Only vehicles of park rangers or other officials are allowed to travel the firebreaks. Furthermore, the road is quite rough, and in some places, impassable. For a vehicle to be "zooming" down this road at 3:00 A.M. is more than unusual—it's extremely dangerous.

The road is about two miles from Dr. Phillips' house. Phillips saw the disk appear much lower and closer, about a half-mile away. Although he didn't see any lights on the object, it was so silvery that it easily reflected all the light around it. As he recalled, "It was directly over the boulevard going down the creek . . . it was just shiny and bright . . . I would hesitate to say glowing. It just looked like it reflected light—a luminous silvery object. It just looked like shiny metal."

He estimated the object was about fifty feet long and about the size of a small house. Although he found it difficult to estimate its speed, Dr. Phillips is certain that it moved at least fifty or sixty miles per hour.

It all happened so quickly, Phillips barely had time to react. The encounter didn't frighten him. "I'm fascinated by it. I think it's eerie. It sort of makes the hair stand up on the back of my neck, but it doesn't make me scared. I want to go find out what it is."

Dr. Phillips doesn't understand why so many people are embarrassed or ashamed to talk about their own UFO sightings. He has no fears at all about telling people what he saw. Though he didn't mention it to his neighbors, he did tell a friend at work. She told another friend, who just happened to be the fellow UFO investigator who referred the case to me. So it was only through a series of coincidences that the report came to light.

Knowing that other people may have seen the same thing, I began calling the other Topanga witnesses to see if they had anything to report.

To my surprise, Roger and Sarah Martin both reported that the UFOs had been coming back again.

They stated that for the last few months, they had been repeatedly awakened between 1:00 and 3:00 A.M. by the strange buzzing sound that they had come to know so well. Although they hadn't actually seen the objects, they know they're out there. Roger reports that the objects had been appearing at least as often as they had the previous year.

When I told them about Dr. Phillips's sighting, they were unable to verify having had any experiences on that evening. However, they also said they heard the UFOs so often, that it could have been on the same evening as Dr. Phillips's sighting.

I was unable to locate any other witnesses to the event; however, less than two months later, another strange encounter came to light. It involved two witnesses who live in northern Topanga Canyon. The encounter occurred on the cloudy evening of November 21, 1993 at about 9:00 P.M. The witnesses desired to remain anonymous. We shall call them Michael and Helen Thompson.

Just prior to the encounter, helicopters had been searching the area. Helen had heard earlier on television that a child was missing and assumed that a search was being conducted in the area. Later that evening, they were watching television. Helen looked out the window and she noticed bright circles of light darting through the clouds.

"There were four of them. They were circling around, and then they'd become like one and sort of bounce off each other and go around in a circle again, and then become one and bounce off each other . . . they were just round circles. It was real cloudy that day

127

and if it had come from the ground we would have seen some sort of rays of light. But they were just lights. They were white lights and there were four of them."

The lights were apparently the size of a full moon, and looked like searchlights except without a beam. Their strange movement was also perplexing. As Helen related, "They never blinked. They joined together and sort of bounced off each other . . . very fast, much faster than any airplane or helicopter could move."

Helen's husband, Michael, agreed with her that the lights were unusual. "It looked like . . . the searchlights they have for the premieres of the movies. They look for planes. You know, when they premiere a movie, they use those big lights? Except that there was no protrusion from the ground. They were just there. And they were spinning around in a circle, three or four of them, real fast, and then they would become one. Then they would separate again from what I remember. They weren't real bright. They were kind of faded out, kind of a whitish faded color. But there was no protrusion from the ground. See . . . it was some kind of spotlight from the ground—that's why we were looking up at it."

As they watched, several planes flew nearby. As Michael said, "We saw planes going by it. I saw some planes flying by it, at the time . . . they were going kind of parallel to it, sideways alongside it at the same height. But they were distinguishable. You could tell that the headlight of the plane was going eastbound towards [the] Burbank airport."

Michael is mystified about what the lights could have been. As he says, "I don't know if they were reflections on the clouds. They were spheres. They were round circles of light . . . you couldn't see where it was coming from. It was just there. You couldn't see if it was coming from above or from below. It was just there. They were just there."

It was the movement that most impressed Michael. "It was a perfect pattern, and it didn't really move as a plane would have to move . . . kind of like a roulette wheel with lights on it, four lights. Picture a wheel and four wheels within a wheel. And the wheel is spinning around with four wheels and all of a sudden, it becomes one wheel in the center of four wheels. And then they separate again and become a wheel with four little wheels, spinning really fast. And that's it. And spinning perfectly level to the ground, not diagonal or anything like that, just level . . . the pattern was really unusual also, the way that the four became one and split up again . . . it was very precise, very symmetrical."

As they watched the lights, both Michael and Helen were convinced they were seeing something very extra-ordinary. As Michael said, "I thought it was unusual. I've never seen anything like it."

After observing them for about twenty minutes, Michael and Helen saw the lights suddenly disappear. As Helen said, "I didn't see how they disappeared because I called my father—he lives next door—to see if he also saw the lights. And while I was in the conversation, I asked my husband a question and he looked back at me. When he looked up in the sky again, they were gone. So we didn't see how they left."

Helen was impressed by the sighting enough to start making some phone calls. "I called KABC and I asked if anybody had reported some lights, and they said no and that they didn't know of anything offhand . . . She said she'd talk with a weather person, but I felt kind of weird about that. I didn't want anybody to think I was a 'nut case' or anything. I didn't know how they would take it . . . I called the *Messenger* to see if anybody else reported it because I knew—I think it was about three or four months ago I read in the newspaper about lights, the ones that people had reported before. I called the sheriff's department because I thought they had some helicopters there earlier, and I just thought, who knows? . . . they said the hunt for the little girl was not in their district and that the Los Angeles Police would know. And then I really discounted the whole thing because I'd seen a couple of helicopters go near the lights, and also a couple of planes, and the lights were just going way much faster than the planes or the helicopters were going."

Helen was unable to gain any new information. When asked if the sighting scared them at all, Helen replied, "No, funny enough, it didn't. I just kind of got the creeps later on. But that day, it was almost pretty to us. We weren't afraid at all . . . it was just so unusual. It could be explained, I'm sure. I didn't feel any fear when I saw those lights, but I've sort of gotten the creeps. But it definitely is unexplainable to me."

Without any prompting, Helen described another mystery that she thought might be related to her sighting. Like many people in Topanga Canyon, Helen boards horses in a stable in her backyard. It was after the sighting that she noticed strange wounds on her horses. She has no idea if the wounds were in any way

130

related to the sighting. She only considered the possibility of a relationship because both events were unexplained and occurred at the same time. "I don't know if it's a coincidence or what, but my horses have been having some unusual wounds—some hair loss really, not so much a wound. And the hair loss is such that the horses couldn't have been rubbing or anything because there are no short hairs around it. It's almost like somebody had waxed a patch of their hair. It's a little bit warm to the touch and the skin is almost leathery. My first horse got this and it took forever to heal. It's been over a month, and for a long time there wasn't even any hair growing there."

Helen is quite familiar with horses and said she's never seen anything like this before. "[It is] a patch of loss of hair, and there's no trauma. So the horse couldn't have rubbed it out. There's kind of blood underneath the skin, but it's not a scab. It's not on top of the skin. The skin hasn't been broken.

"I showed it to some people, and one girl who has her horse here said, 'Gee, it looks like the horse has just been waxed or something.' It's kind of unusual. And then I asked a doctor who boards his horse here, and he said, 'Well, I don't know. It looks kind of unusual. It could be mites.' But it hasn't spread. She doesn't have it on any other part of her body, just this one patch. And I didn't brush the hair off. That's usually what happens with mites or some parasites—you brush your horse and then the hair falls off. It was a very, very clean patch . . . it's right on her face, right on her nose, on the side of her face. It's about a half-dollar . . . I know I'm kind of jumping the gun on this. The only reason why I thought of that was because my dog acted a little bit strange lately at nighttime, and I thought it was unusual that I just happened to look out the window and see these lights. I thought that maybe they had come around at a time when I didn't see them."

Two of the horses Helen boarded had marks appear on them. One mark appeared about a month prior to the sighting. The other appeared shortly after that. Helen was alarmed when she saw the second wound, not only because it was identical to the first one, but because the first wound had failed to heal. "It took a very long time for the hair to grow back," she explained. "Usually within a couple of days, if a horse has an injury or something, the hair starts growing back. The hair didn't grow back. I mean, it didn't even start to stubble or anything like that for at least a month."

The first horse's wound was on its face. On the second horse, the wound was on the neck. As Helen related, "The same shape, and pretty much the same [wound]. I thought it was really unusual that she got it too, because there was nothing unusual happening around [the place]. I just thought, 'Well, it's something unexplainable. It will heal up. No big deal.'"

Although there is no direct evidence to link the wounds on the horses to the objects, in other UFO hotspots, animal mutilations have been reported. Certainly it is possible that something similar happened in this case. However, this is pure speculation. It is also interesting that Helen noticed her dog behaving strangely. As we have seen, animals often react strangely to UFO encounters.

With these new cases, the Topanga encounters began to take on a new dimension. What seemed to be a short wave of UFO activity turned out to be a long-running series of dramatic encounters. The more I investigated, the more encounters I uncovered. I found cases that had occurred decades earlier, and cases that were literally in the process of happening. Some of these turned out to be the most mind-boggling yet.

12

"Encounters" Visits Topanga

Topanga Canyon had become a UFO hotspot. I had investigated the area and uncovered the entire range of encounters. The only thing left to do was to try to capture the objects on film. I had already done several UFO stakeouts in Topanga, but the time had come for a new approach. I had joined the Center for the Study of Extraterrestrial Intelligence (CSETI) founded by Dr. Steven Greer, M.D. CSETI's basic premise is that UFOs should be studied live in the field, as opposed to researched after the fact. Using various methods, CSETI strives to initiate an encounter and open the lines of communication between UFOs and their witnesses. This unique and controversial idea seemed perfect for Topanga.

There are many cases of this type on record. I personally investigated two such cases. One occurred at the George Page Museum, at the La Brea Tar Pits in Santa Monica; strange objects were attracted to very bright lights that had been laid out on the front lawn in the shape of a disk. Another occurred in San Diego; an object was attracted to the beam of a 25-watt green argon laser, which was being used as a publicity stunt. These two cases are covered in my earlier book, *One In Forty: The UFO Epidemic*. I knew that it should be possible to initiate an encounter in Topanga Canyon.

The local LA–CSETI group (formed in August 1992, shortly after the Topanga UFO wave began) had already ventured into Topanga several times but with very limited success. Still, I knew that because the activity in the area was so high, it was only a matter of time before somebody sighted an object and photographed it.

Then came wonderful news. The television program *Encounters: The Hidden Truth* had heard about CSETI's unique approach to UFO research and wanted to do a segment on the subject. When they heard Topanga was a UFO hotspot—literally in their backyard—the pieces began to fall into place.

In July, 1994 *Encounters* sent a crew to interview me about my involvement with CSETI and my investigations into the Topanga Canyon sightings and encounters. Several hours later, we all headed out into Topanga for what would turn out to be a remarkably successful adventure.

About ten of us met in the State Park at dusk. The crew from *Encounters* arrived with several vans of equipment. After a quick supper, we left the parking lot of Trippett Ranch and hiked a couple of hundred yards northwest into the fields. The television crew kept their huge camera trained on us as we settled into our spot and began the protocols. CSETI uses several methods to contact UFOs including lights, sounds, and meditative techniques. All these methods have proved successful in other cases.

On this particular occasion, *Encounters* had hired somebody to operate a laser. Normally we use half-million-watt flashlights to attract the attention of UFOs. These were brought to the site and the crew filmed a few of us doing what we call "light work." Finally, it was time to set up the laser.

The laser needed the power of a generator that was in one of the crew's vans. But the laser itself was actually quite small; four feet long and six inches wide. It was thrilling to see the beam cut through the night air. Mist was beginning to form, but still the night was clear. The laser operator moved the beam in different patterns and flashed different colors. The crew filmed the sequence and the laser was shut off.

We continued doing the protocols, which included playing recordings of UFO beeping sounds supplied by CSETI from an actual case, meditation techniques, and keeping a sharp lookout for any unusual activity. *Encounters* was preparing to film the closing sequence when somebody spotted something unusual on the west horizon over Henry Ridge. The cry of alarm spread through the group and everybody stood and looked to the west. Clearly visible was a bright orangish-white light hovering just above the ridgeline. We all stood watching it. I took my binoculars and looked at the light. I saw the light close up, but was unable to see any wing lights that would betray a plane. Still I knew that it could be a plane. Slowly the light sank behind the ridge.

Conversation began to rumble through the camp. What was it? Could it have been a UFO? Seconds later the light was back. This time, the *Encounters* crew quickly trained their camera on the light and began filming. The light behaved in the same way, hovering for a few seconds, perhaps a minute, and then sank below the horizon.

I remember being somewhat excited, but not too much. I wanted the light to come back, to come closer. And yet, that was to be the end of the encounter. However the UFO had taken *Encounters* by surprise. They later confessed that they had not expected to be successful and so had to change the way they were going to film the end of the segment. For that reason, they took a few moments before returning to our group with the camera. To my horror, they trained the camera on me and asked me point blank, "Well, Preston, what did we see? Did we see a UFO?"

I said, "We prefer to call them unknowns. This sort of thing has happened before. Now, if it had been a closer encounter, that would have been a different story. Still I'm pretty excited. I'm pleased."

Later on I was to have a much more vivid sighting in Topanga while leading the CSETI group. The sighting with *Encounters,* however, turned out to be more successful than we could have hoped. Although it was only a sighting of an anomalous light, it is significant for several reasons. Not only was CSETI perhaps able to initiate a UFO encounter, but *Encounters* actually caught the object on film. The segment played in mid-October and showed a few seconds of the light hovering over the ridge. Although you can't see much, there are over a dozen witnesses who will tell you that the light was actually there and was quite bright. Another significant aspect of this sighting is the fact that it took place in Topanga, proving once again that Topanga Canyon is a hotspot of major proportions.

A few months after the *Encounters* adventure, the local KTLA Channel 13 Evening News heard about CSETI's work and they wanted to do a story. Again, a slightly smaller group of LA–CSETI members met in Topanga State Park. We performed the CSETI protocols while the television crew filmed a short segment. Unfortunately, nothing appeared for the cameras.

Nineteen ninety-four would still turn out to be a very busy year for the Topanga UFOs. Before the *Encounters* segment, I had already uncovered several encounters. Throughout the year, new witnesses came forth with new encounters. I also began to receive more encounters from the communities directly bordering Topanga Canyon.

13

Sightings in
Santa Monica

ALTHOUGH THE MAJORITY
of the UFO encounters were concentrated over
Topanga Canyon, it was only because Topanga is in
the heart of the Santa Monica mountain range. The
borders of Topanga Canyon do not cover the entire
mountain range. Topanga is sandwiched between
Santa Monica and Malibu, both of which are partially
contained in the Santa Monica mountain range.

Since the borders between any two places are often
largely arbitrary, one would expect that neighboring
areas such as Santa Monica and Malibu would also
have a large number of encounters. As it turned out,
this was exactly the case. It seems the objects were
drawn to the Santa Monica mountain range as a
whole, and not just Topanga Canyon.

The first reports from outside Topanga Canyon
came from Santa Monica. East of Topanga Canyon,
Santa Monica is only partially located in the Santa
Monica Mountains. However, it is precisely in this

area where the UFOs have been seen. To date, well over a dozen people have had encounters of various types there.

One of the most dramatic encounters occurred early one summer evening in 1980. Donald and Bonnie, their three children, and two neighbors all became witnesses to a remarkable encounter. They were able to observe an anomalous object for over ten minutes using a pair of high-powered binoculars. Even with the binoculars, however, they were unable to identify exactly what it was they were observing.

As Bonnie related, "We all came outside and looked at it. In fact, my husband saw it and my other two kids saw it too. But what it was—we were outside and we saw this thing in the sky that was absolutely quiet and it was just hovering. It wasn't a helicopter or anything because there was no noise. It was a red light and it was the shape of a half-pie pan, like a half-circle. And it was red. It was out there long enough that the next door neighbors came out and looked at it too. And we got the binoculars out . . . we had no idea what it was. We just kept saying, 'What on Earth could it possibly be if there's no noise and it's just hovering?'"

Bonnie's husband, Donald, was similarly impressed. "We just don't know what it was, which I guess is what a UFO is. But we went outside and we looked up in the sky. I don't remember who saw it first. It appeared to be stationary. As I recall, it was red with slight greens in it, but mostly red. And we watched it for the longest time, got out the binoculars. It was far too high to be a helicopter, but I can't tell you how high it was. It didn't appear to be a star and it wasn't a plane. We have a lot of planes that go over here. It stayed in the same place . . . it was a lot brighter than anything else around. I knew it wasn't Mars because my son was into astronomy at the time and Mars wasn't anywhere near there."

As Bonnie watched, she noticed an important detail—the object or light actually swayed back and forth as it silently hovered. She, like many UFO witnesses, had great trouble estimating the altitude of the object. Then, without warning, the object suddenly streaked away. As Bonnie recalled, "We don't know how far away it was. I know that it's never been there before or since. We know our sky, what is up near our house. If I were to judge, I would say it was about as high as a helicopter might be. It did kind of move around a little tiny bit, but mainly it just hovered. It moved like a bit from side to side, but it didn't go anywhere until it was just gone . . . it's just like it just went away."

Donald also saw the object abruptly leave. "It kind of just went away. No noise. It just went away. . . ."

They had no idea what the object could have been. As Bonnie explained, "Nobody knew what that was. We had never seen anything like that before."

This report is important for many reasons. Several adults were able to observe the object for over ten minutes with the aid of binoculars. These conditions strongly reduce the possibility that the sighting was the result of the misperception of an ordinary object.

Also, the witnesses describe many of the details that are typical of UFO reports, including the difficulty of estimating size and distance, the strange rocking motion, the complete silence, and the rapid departure. These and other details are important clues to the veracity of a UFO encounter.

Bonnie and Donald received further verification of their sighting when, two days later, Bonnie's parents reported seeing an identical object. Bonnie's parents both witnessed a red object in the shape of a half-circle hovering outside their own home in the neighboring city of Mar Vista.

Bonnie and Donald were surprised to hear how closely Bonnie's parents' account matched their own. Bonnie related, "My parents live five miles away from me. I live in Santa Monica. They live in Mar Vista. They saw the same thing. And their neighbors went out and looked at it. And nobody knew what it was. So in that sense, it was unidentified. It was described just like ours, the red thing—it was red, like red lights."

The above encounter is a perfect illustration of how the Topanga UFOs behave. Not only did the object hover for at least ten minutes in full view of several adults using binoculars, but it returned two days later for a repeat performance. It is as if the objects have no fear whatsoever of being observed. In fact, it is as if they want to be observed; as if they are putting on a display.

This theory was supported when I received another report of a red object over the Santa Monica mountains, from pilot and flight instructor Toshi Inouye. He regularly trains students along the coast and over the Santa Monica Mountains.

On one particular occasion in 1980, he and a student encountered a huge red object hovering low over the mountains. It was around 5:00 P.M. and the sun was still shining. Inouye was busy pointing out the instrument readings to his student and teaching him how to fly. They were at about two thousand feet heading east towards the Santa Monica Airport when they noticed a large red object hovering to their left about two miles away, directly over the Santa Monica Mountains.

As a pilot, Inouye is not only trained to identify flying craft, but has considerable experience in this area. So when he saw the huge red object, he knew instantly that it was unusual. Even though he could see it clearly, he simply could not figure out what it was. He tried to describe it. "This one was cigar-shaped. It was red. It was glowing red in the shape of a cigar. That was after we made contact with the tower, and we got clearance to get into airport traffic to Santa Monica Airport. We were at about the shoreline of Santa Monica Beach to Pacific Palisades. Usually the tower advises us of other traffic next to us. But they didn't, right? So I grabbed the other microphone, and I was going to ask if there was any other traffic nearby."

At this point, Inouye hesitated. Did he really want to call up and report a UFO? "We were looking about twenty seconds or thirty seconds. It was standing still in the air, glowing red. We were kind of stunned. We didn't know what to do. The next thing I was going to do was pick up the microphone and ask the tower. But we didn't. I'm glad I didn't ask anything because it was kind of . . . asking if there was any other object that looks like a flying saucer?"

Although the light was not very far away, neither Inouye nor his student was able to discern if the object was a solid object or just a light. Inouye said, "This one looked like a light, but it looked like a shiny, shiny light, though. It showed the shape of it, but it wasn't a bright light. I couldn't see any detail of it, just a kind of reddish cigar shape. It was a cigar-shaped light."

Inouye and his student then watched the object leave. Like most UFOs, it departed instantaneously. Inouye continued, "He was looking at it. I was looking at it. And then, all of a sudden, it disappeared. It disappeared while we were looking at it, which means that the object moved away with a very, very fast speed."

Inouye estimated that the object was about "two to three times bigger than a bus." Even though he has been a pilot for over twenty years, he had no idea what the object was.

Again, there was an additional sighting a few days later. Inouye's student told him that two days after the sighting, he and several friends had another encounter that was much more dramatic. Inouye's student said he and several friends not only saw the same object, but that it actually chased their car for several miles along the twisting mountain roads. As Inouye described it, "This student was in a car driving over the Santa Monica Mountains with his friends, a couple of other friends. He stated that he was chased by the object. According to him, the object looked like it was following the car. They were driving. According to him, it was the same one. At least for him, the object looked like the same shape we saw in the airplane."

Whether or not the above witnesses all observed the same UFO is, of course, a matter of speculation. All that is known is that these people are seeing *something* very unusual. The question is what *is* it?

The above witnesses all report seeing just a red light. Although the light remains unidentified, nothing was seen that could be conclusively called an actual craft; a red light hardly qualifies as an alien spaceship.

However, there is at least one report from Santa Monica that fits the description of an alien spaceship exactly. This report involves an extremely close-up sighting of a metallic, disk-shaped craft.

The main witness is a gentleman involved in the film industry as an artist. He has worked on the sets of *Star Trek: The Motion Picture* and *Star Trek: The Next Generation*. Because of his career and because his encounter is so incredible, he elected to remain anonymous. We have given him the pseudonym of George Gray. George was referred to me by another Topanga Canyon UFO witness.

It was the week after Easter in 1975, when George was moving into the Los Angeles area. He, his sister, and her boyfriend packed George's belongings into two cars and began the drive into Los Angeles. They left at around 5:00 A.M. George drove alone and the other two followed in another car. They turned north on the San Diego Freeway and then turned west onto the Santa Monica Freeway.

It was so early that it was still dark and the stars were out. Traffic was extremely light and they made excellent time.

George had seen what he believes were UFOs on a few occasions earlier in his life. Although very brief, the sightings fascinated him, so he always kept his eyes open hoping to catch another glimpse. Usually, of course, nothing appeared. But on this particular morning, George was not to be disappointed.

As they raced down the Santa Monica Freeway, George suddenly noticed a round, glowing object darting back and forth across the sky, sending down beams of light. Although the object was obviously strange, it didn't yet dawn on George that he was seeing an actual UFO.

George reported, "I noticed towards the west what I thought at first was a helicopter, because helicopters have spotlights, you know. It was over the ocean. But all of a sudden, I noticed that the light just zoomed towards Palos Verdes at a tremendous rate of speed and then zoomed right back. That blew me away and I thought, 'Wait a minute. This is just moving too fast.' And then I noticed when it stopped, it sent a beam of light down.

"I know helicopters have spotlights, but this was an incredibly different type of light. It was like a cylinder of light being actually lowered down, like a cylinder. I have never seen light ever do that before. Most light will scatter. This light stayed uniform completely, like a cylinder would be lowered down. And the light was a brilliant bluish-green light. I could see the beach where the wet sand would be because it illuminated it. And within this cylinder of light, it would send smaller cylinders of light within it. And those were even brilliant, like a yellow-lime-green and an orange cylinder also within this other cylinder.

"I was seeing this and I said, 'Whoa!' I knew right then and there that I was witnessing a UFO. I am familiar with aircraft and satellites and all that due to the fact that my dad worked on the Apollo space program. I attended astronomy classes in high school, so I'm familiar with the planet Venus, the moon and all that, and satellites. I'm knowledgeable about airplanes and aircraft and helicopters. So I knew what I saw was a UFO."

At this point, George became very excited. He had always wanted to see a UFO close-up, and now it looked like it was actually happening. He automatically began sending out thoughts of love to the UFO. Then he honked his car horn wildly and pointed out the object to his sister and friend. Around this time, they reached the end of the Santa Monica Freeway and went through the McClure Tunnel that leads to the Pacific Coast Highway and into Topanga Canyon. As soon as they exited the short tunnel and reached the beach, they pulled off the road and began to carefully observe the object, which was now quite close.

As George recalled, "I was waiting to pull over to make a left onto where the beach was. And we finally did. We pulled over and the UFO followed us . . . I jumped out of the van and started walking towards it. The UFO was over where the beach was, where the wet sand would be, hovering, I would say maybe a hundred, two hundred feet in the air. It was silver. It was your basic UFO, like two saucer shapes.

"It was a light at first," George explained, "because it was still dark. Now when we finally got there, the sun had started to come up. But it was definitely completely metallic with a silver dome on the top and a silver dome on the bottom of it, like two plates put together. And they had little lights around it."

The three witnesses stood on the beach and watched with rapt fascination for at least ten minutes. All of them were completely awestruck. The metallic craft floated lazily up and down the beach, casting down a solid-looking beam of light at various seemingly random intervals. At one point, it scared away a flock of seagulls.

All at once, they realized the sun had risen and traffic was definitely increasing. At the moment the sun had fully risen, the object instantly departed. As George described it, "Just like that, it just took off straight up."

After the object left, George was so excited, he was literally jumping up and down. All three of them were totally amazed to have seen the object so close-up. George said, "It was really something to see. The craft, I would say, in size was maybe a hundred feet across or so. It was a relatively big craft that I saw and it was completely metallic . . . it was definitely a silver, metallic object that I saw, and shiny. And once the sun was breaking through, you could really see beautifully buffed, almost mirror, liquid mirror, like mercury, metallic—that's what I'm trying to explain. The object was highly buffed."

Like many UFO witnesses, George felt that there may have been some type of communication with the object. "It hovered there and it acknowledged that we were there . . . but then it just took off, straight up. We could see it. It didn't just disappear. It went shew! It just took off."

George reported that at one point the object definitely followed his car and actually seemed to show off. "I really believe that it came back when I started trying to use communication, telepathy. Because it came back and when I pulled over, it was there."

George was deeply impressed by the sighting and says that it was definitely the most dramatic UFO encounter he has ever had.

14

The Malibu Sightings

JUST WEST OF Topanga Canyon, Malibu lies almost entirely within the Santa Monica mountains. Due to this proximity, there was a high probability that Malibu was also generating a large number of UFO reports. After investigating Topanga Canyon and Santa Monica, I knew that Malibu was the next logical step. I expected to find Malibu had more encounters than Santa Monica, but less than Topanga Canyon. This turned out to be exactly the case.

Malibu, like Topanga, has had the entire range of UFO encounters, from unexplained lights and metallic ships, to UFO landings and missing-time abductions.

One of the first people to reveal his story was Malibu resident Eric Beckjord. Eric is no stranger to the unexplained, and is a UFO researcher. When he had his own sighting of a UFO over Malibu, he didn't hesitate to report it. Soon after the sighting, he spoke before an audience of about fifty people from a Los Angeles MUFON group, revealing the details of his sighting. He was also gracious enough to grant me a personal interview.

The sighting took place one night in October, 1992, right in the heart of Malibu. Eric reported, "I was driving home at approximately 10:00 P.M. It was a couple of miles up Las Flores Canyon Road. And I saw that about five miles further at the top of the mountain range, there was a fuzzy, bright light that was moving kind of like a fly buzzing, kind of like an insect buzzing along the top of the ridges, following the contours of the ridges. It was basically a very bright light that was pulsing. It would go from bright down to weak and return to bright again."

Eric knew instantly that he was looking at something unusual. "It had no markings. It had no lights that were similar to a helicopter or any conventional aircraft. No green lights, no red lights, no strobing light. The entire thing would be bright and then would go down to dim and then bright again. It never completely went off."

Eric estimates the "blob of light" to be about forty feet across or about the size of a small house. As he watched the object move silently over the mountains, his first impulse was to dash down to his house and get his camera. Immediately, the object departed. Eric recalled, "As I was thinking that, it kind of went over the edge of a ridge and disappeared."

Eric was so impressed by the sighting that he called up the Malibu fire department and reported his sighting. Although the fire department hadn't received any other calls, Eric was sure he saw something unusual. "At the other end of the canyon, down where it goes into the water, we have a tremendous amount of aircraft activity to and from LAX. And I see aircraft constantly. This did not appear to be one of those. And it was also very much out of the flight pattern."

Eric Beckjord's sighting has many of the trademarks of other accounts in the area. An equally, if not more astonishing report of unexplained lights over the Santa Monica Mountains occurred on May 26 and 27, 1993 to Malibu residents Chuck and Karen, who live along a ridgetop off Kanan Road.

On May 26, Karen was home alone, laying in bed and watching the stars outside their picture window. It was around 9:00 P.M. when she noticed some movement up in the sky. To her astonishment, at about forty-five degrees above the western horizon, she saw a bright star-like object surrounded by several red lights. As she watched, the light began zigzagging quickly across the sky.

Karen remembered, "It just kind of danced up; it would go up and then fall, coming down to the side. It did kind of an erratic dance pattern is how you would describe it. And then it had all these red lights sometimes. They kind of varied and they would shoot off and it would look almost like a whip, almost like a whip effect. Then when Chuck got home, we started looking and we started seeing more of them. We probably saw a total of six or seven. But the first one we saw was the strongest one. And the other ones were a little harder to spot. You had to look. But they were all doing the same thing."

Karen watched the lights for almost three hours before Chuck finally came home. By then, she had observed the lights long enough to conclude that she was seeing something unexplainable. "It looked like a star. The only thing that didn't look like a star was the stuff that was coming off of it. That was especially what was unusual. It was like there was three lights that would be around the main light, and the three lights—I think that number would vary—but they would seem to keep a certain distance from the center one, and they would also blink and they would reappear somewhere else in that area. And like I said, there was that whip of light or something coming off the big one, which was really like small lines of red lights."

By the time Chuck came home, Karen had stopped staring at the lights, but only checked periodically to see if they were still there. She told Chuck about the lights and he became instantly intrigued. He turned off all the house lights and looked where Karen was pointing.

He was shocked by what he saw. "We started laying down and looking up at the sky, and what she was pointing at—it took me just a second to see it—was something that appeared to be a star in the sky. She had talked about these long red lines following it. What appeared to be a star was then being—my description is a whole bunch of small red lights that would wing around some direction . . . and the thing that kept showing up that made it so unusual to me was this winging of—I would say it could be a half-dozen to ten or fifteen red lights that would go out. And if you were taking a drape or something and shaking it, or a sheet in the wind, it would leave a trail. Or if a dancer were dancing around in a circle and she were leaving a trail. It was really like something was whipping these trails of lights around. And they would go way up, way up, and then fall back down around it. And then they would disappear and you'd see the erratic movement of the star. And then you'd watch them come out again.

Chuck was very careful about what he was observing. "The size of the lights was star-size. The one we noticed most was like a fairly dim star in the sky, but there was no question it was being trailed around with this erratic movement that appeared to be having some geometric reason. The red lights, the way they would just go and then kind of come back and shoot way up into the sky and then fall down and then kind of disappear. . . ."

To make sure they weren't imagining the movement, Chuck and Karen used an ingenious technique. "This was how we knew," Karen explained. "We held up a piece of paper against the glass that was steady, and we steadied ourselves against it so that you wouldn't wiggle at all. And then you could actually see the thing moving against the straight line of the paper . . . another thing why we were really convinced that they were moving as much as they were moving is because when we were both looking at it from different angles as we were sitting there, we could both describe the movements. We saw, we'd say, 'Oh, now it's falling to the right!' And we would both agree we were seeing the exact same thing."

Although they both knew they were seeing something unusual, they were still reluctant to admit it. Chuck said, "I kept thinking, 'I wonder what this is?' Then the thing that freaked me out and left me uneasy the most was when another bright light just took off way up in the sky and just took off. And that's the thing that defined the experience as something very different. All of a sudden, there was a white light that started to do something, and it was right next to it and took off. So if something were to move at the speed of light, that thing moved as fast as I have ever seen anything move in the sky. It was really unusual and we did watch it quite a bit."

It was around 1:00 A.M. that Chuck and Karen finally decided to call the Malibu Sheriff's Station. The officer on duty told them that there had been no other reports that night, and that the police don't handle UFO reports. The officer referred them to me and I received Chuck's call a few minutes later, as the encounter was still in progress.

I did a quick preliminary interview to assess the story, and then got their address. After hanging up, my brother and I drove to the location of the incident hopefully to observe the objects. Unfortunately, we didn't see anything. We drove back home disappointed.

The next day I called Chuck and Karen. They said that after they called me, they went back and continued observing the lights for several more minutes. By this time it was quite late, so even though the lights were still in the sky, they went to sleep.

The next evening, on May 27, the objects returned. Karen said, "We looked the next night again after that and there was the same thing . . . we haven't really seen them again since, but we did see them two nights in a row, and they weren't in the exact same spot. It looked like they moved over to the left the next night. They were still in view of our window."

Chuck was more reluctant than Karen to admit that the UFOs had actually returned again. In fact, he says the idea scares him. "The next night, we came back in and looked, and you kind of want to see the same thing in a way. You do and you don't. I was a little bit kind of worried to look . . . so we turned off all the lights and we looked. And sure enough if it didn't look like we could see the same thing. But right now, I don't know. I thought I saw the same thing again . . . I just know that what we saw that first night was something that I had noticed in the sky that I never noticed before."

Chuck's and Karen's reluctance to examine the objects on the second night may seem strange, but it is a common reaction of UFO witnesses. Neither of them had seen UFOs before, and the idea that something unknown is flying around at night can be a little disconcerting. As Chuck admitted, "The second night we didn't pay a lot of attention to it because we thought . . . you know, it's a little bit scary to think that something's sitting out there. And I started to think, 'Well, maybe this is something I don't know about.'"

Chuck and Karen delicately asked their neighbors about recent UFO sightings, but none of them had seen anything. They set up a small telescope in case the lights returned. However, they have not since had any further sightings.

Malibu has had other impressive reports of unexplained lights. Many of the sightings have occurred along the coast, over the Santa Monica Bay and Santa Catalina Channel.

Tony has lived in Malibu for many years. He owns a home along the Pacific Coast Highway and has a wonderful view of the Santa Monica Bay. Tony is somewhat skeptical of UFOs. However, one evening early in 1991, at about 3:00 or 4:00 A.M., Tony happened to be awake, and looked out his ocean-front window. To his puzzlement, he saw a brilliantly lit object apparently floating on the ocean's surface about two miles away. At first the light didn't seem strange. However, as he looked more carefully, Tony saw that the light had a strange shape and was emitting remarkably vivid colors.

Tony described it: "It looked just like a big prism, kind of various colors out there. I got a telescope out there and looked at it, and although it's a thirty-power telescope, when I looked at it [closely], it even seemed more like a prism, just different colors."

After watching it for several minutes, the lights "winked" out. Although Tony didn't know what the light was, he didn't associate it with a UFO. Two years later, in January, 1993, the glowing prism returned. Again it appeared to be a diamond-shaped light flashing vivid colors while floating on the ocean's surface. Tony again examined the object with his telescope. The vivid colors made him speculate that a boat might be on fire.

"I got the telescope and looked at it," Tony said. "and it was the same kind of thing. So I called the Coast Guard and asked them. I thought perhaps it might be a fire because of the different colors and that kind of thing, and they said that they hadn't had any reports. And they suggested one possibility for this thing was that the squid fishermen use these big booms with lights on them to attract fish to the surface. And it may have been that although I don't know . . . there will never be a way for me to figure out what the hell this was out there."

Tony told the Coast Guard he thought a ship might be burning and they explained flatly, "We can rule out fire," and stuck to the squid explanation. The person on duty then admitted to Tony, "I'm kind of reluctant to scramble an aircraft because it's probably that squid thing."

Tony told them he would continue to observe the light. He noticed that even with the telescope, he was unable to get any more detail and that the object didn't even look closer. Tony decided that it probably wasn't a boat on fire, but he still couldn't understand what was causing the vivid colors. "The more I thought about it, it had that kind of flickering quality, but the colors didn't seem right for a fire . . . I thought that there was a wind that was probably rippling the ocean, and maybe that's what I was seeing. But the colors seemed so—what would the word be? . . . pure, for lack of a better word. They seemed real coherent."

After several minutes, the light winked out. Tony called the Coast Guard and gave his report. He is not convinced that he saw a UFO. "I would be tempted to believe that probably it was the 'squid thing,' although the colors were so bright. Because, who knows? With halogen lights, which is probably what they were using, if that's what it is, it could bounce some outrageous colors off the water."

Unfortunately, Tony's sighting remains a mystery. It may have been caused by squid fishermen, but it is odd that Tony has only seen the light twice in all the years he has lived in Malibu. He jokingly admitted the possibility that both explanations could be correct; maybe the light was caused by alien fishermen. "They caught the squid they needed for that night, whoever they are. Maybe Gladstones has a deal with UFO people to get squid. 'Here you go, we'll trade you cattle for squid!'"

Although Tony's sighting is open to conventional explanations, other sightings are not as easy to explain away.

One such sighting involves Anthony, who saw a star-like object over Topanga with three other people in 1992. Anthony is a contactee, and has seen UFOs on many occasions. He has also had one-on-one communications with extraterrestrials. He was given a telepathic message that UFOs would appear on July 14, 1992. He was told that he should get in view of the ocean if he wanted to see a "display."

After Anthony had his sighting in Topanga State Park, he drove down to Malibu. He and a friend sneaked into Charmlee Park at night, after it had closed. Just as Anthony had been told, the UFOs appeared. Anthony and his friend saw and photographed several glowing tear-shaped objects which were performing strange maneuvers over the ocean.

As Anthony remembered, "What's interesting is that there were several of them, I think, four or five of them . . . it started off as a point on the ocean horizon where the shore came in. And it took a long time. It wasn't a very fast thing. It took a long time to go across and just went right on going . . . it was a very strange sighting. It wasn't a real close sighting. It was off in the distance, on the horizon. It was a lighted object, but it was more pointed. You couldn't tell if it was solid at all. It was a sort of sparkling light. That's what I call it, a sparkly type. There were no visible lights to it, nothing blinking on and off. It was just a really neat little thing."

The objects were in view for about an hour. When they finally left, they moved in such a way that removed any doubt that they might have a conventional explanation. Anthony said, "They did a loop! . . . They went along the horizon, did a little loop, and then went. They kept on going." While the objects had been in view, Anthony's friend took several photographs of the objects. Unfortunately, the quality of the photos was very poor.

The Santa Catalina Channel is the location of yet another report of anomalous lights. This sighting involved two witnesses. One of them, Linda Susan Young, lives in Santa Monica where she works as a therapist. In June, 1980, she and a friend decided to go out for dinner. It was just after sunset when they headed north on the Pacific Coast Highway.

Linda was sitting in the passenger seat talking when she noticed what appeared to be a light floating on the water. As she says, "I was talking to the driver, so I was facing the ocean. And it took a while before it dawned on me that I was seeing something. It was just sort of there. And all of a sudden I thought, 'What is that and why is it there?' But at first I just wasn't really conscious of it. While I was talking to him, I was trying to figure out what it was. And I knew the land, where it zigs and zags, that it didn't jut out that far. My sister used to live in Malibu for years and I was up and down, up and down the coast all the time. And I knew it didn't go out that far. And I knew that it was much too far for it to be any kind of oil rig or anything."

As she watched the light, Linda realized something else that seemed strange. "There was some reason I knew it wasn't a ship, I mean a boat-ship, but I can't remember now why I knew that. There was some specific reason I knew . . . it was right on the horizon line. It was just a light. It was a white light and that was all. I didn't see any definition of anything else. For the size of the light, it's like I should have been able to see some sort of definition . . . I couldn't figure out what this would be. And I said to the guy with me, 'What do you suppose this is?' And he turned around and looked at it. And he saw it only for a second when it just shot straight up on the air and blinked out. It didn't look like it went far enough to disappear from view, like from a distance. It just sort of stopped. It just stopped being there."

The movement and disappearance of the light took Linda completely by surprise. Boats weren't supposed to fly up into the sky and disappear. "At the time, I didn't even know what I was looking at. And I didn't expect it to jump up in the air. I really wasn't prepared for this. It went up in the air, but not far enough if it was the climb of distance that it would have disappeared from view, that I would cease to see it. It went up and then I stopped seeing it any further, like it went out."

Linda is certain that the object was not a flare. It was much too large and had been floating on the ocean for several minutes. And it couldn't be explained as a conventional aircraft because the movement was much too quick. Linda described it as "extremely fast. I mean, it was obviously not a helicopter or anything I have ever seen like that in the sky. Like I said, I live next to the Santa Monica airport. I see planes constantly. I'm just two blocks from it. And it was a straight line, straight up, extremely fast."

Linda also remarked how strange it was that the object moved at the exact moment she told her friend to look. "It was sitting there for a few minutes before that happened, because all that time, I was trying to figure out what that was, and it was right when I told him to look at it. I don't know if that had anything to do with it. It could have been just a coincidence that when he turned around, that's when it left."

Is this just a coincidence? Of course, any answer would be speculative. However, the detail may be important because, as we have seen, many other witnesses had reported telepathic communication with UFOs.

What does Linda think she saw? "I have always assumed it was a UFO, but it was sort of a distant view and I didn't see any shape or have any other information about it. But I don't know what else that would have been. Sort of by the process of elimination. . . ."

All these accounts are of unexplained lights at night. It is much rarer to see a solid, metallic-looking object. It is even rarer to see them during full daylight hours. However, this event has occurred in Malibu at least twice.

One incident occurred in 1989, and involved two witnesses, one of whom was Linda Susan Young.

She and her friend, whom we will call Gregory, had been invited to a party at a friend's home in Malibu. Like many homes in Malibu, this home was large and expensive. It was located high on a mountain top in the middle of Malibu. Attending the party was Jao Pio, a well-known contactee and channeler.

On this particular day, Pio was not discussing his UFO experiences, but was channeling music. Linda and Gregory were sitting outside with about twenty other people, listening to Pio play the piano. The sun was shining, but it was near sunset. Suddenly the two of them noticed a strange, metallic object moving slowly northwards between the steep canyon walls, where no plane could go.

As Linda remembered, "I was looking from one side of the canyon to the other. We could see the other side so I know that there was a scooped out space between us . . . the sun was still out, but it was just at sunset, and we saw an object. And as far as I know, it was just Gregory and me. And we're in agreement that it was the size of a very small plane, either like one of these little jets, or something like the size of a glider, like the expanse of a hang-glider or something. It was not real large. I believe that it was metallic-looking, but we didn't even particularly get a shape to it. We were looking at it. It was a horizontal shape. I don't know that you'd call it a cigar-shape or whatever. Because if you were looking exactly level with an airplane, you wouldn't see the wings because they would be sticking out straight at you. So we're not sure what we were seeing because it could have been at the angle where the features were hidden."

Neither Linda nor Gregory saw any wings, windows or markings. It was simply an oval-shaped metallic object. However, as Linda pointed out, the object could have had wings that were hard to see. As a general rule, UFOs not only have a strange appearance, they also move strangely. This was certainly true in this case. As Linda recalled, "We only saw it briefly and it was going very, very slowly. It was just about level with our view in this area, which would have been in the canyon part. But it would have been extremely dangerous for an actual airplane to have been in there because it wasn't that wide. And there was no sound associated with that. And like I said, it was going extremely slowly and in an exact straight line. It didn't waver at all. It didn't bounce around as if something was supporting it like an air current. And we just sort of looked at each other and said, 'Did you see that?' 'Yes!' We were in agreement, but by then it was out of our view."

Gregory's memory of the event matches closely with Linda's. "I was the one there with Linda . . . there was an object flying along the canyon floor, I guess in the valley, very low and very slow . . . there were hills on either side, but there was quite a bit of an opening there and you could see it going across the Pacific Coast Highway towards the valley . . . it was pretty low for a plane. The speed didn't seem to make any sense. I can't see anyone flying any plane down that low."

Unfortunately, the two of them saw the object for only a few seconds before it moved out of view. They thought about jumping up to see more, but they didn't want to disturb the musical performance taking place.

Linda said, "We weren't sure what we had seen. We didn't want to be disruptive. Nobody else seemed to see anything. But we were aware that this man supposedly is in contact with celestial beings."

What did Linda and Gregory see? Could it have been a helicopter, plane, or blimp? A careful examination of their testimonies makes it obvious that no conventional aircraft can account for all the details of their sighting. What could move slowly and steadily between steep canyon walls in perfect silence? Both Linda and Gregory are convinced they saw a UFO. They only wish they could have seen it a little closer.

Another daylight sighting of a solid, metallic-looking craft occurred over Malibu, near Latigo Canyon Road. It was witnessed by Adam and Mario, both in their twenties. Adam is a pool-cleaner and college student, and Mario had recently been discharged from the military. Both are residents of the San Fernando Valley.

On August 16, 1992, just before sunset, Adam and Mario were driving south along the Pacific Coast Highway on their way back from Zuma Beach, when Mario noticed something strange in the sky. Several black diamond-shaped objects were hovering in formation, glinting in the sunlight. Almost instantly, the objects began performing incredible maneuvers.

Adam remembers the event vividly. "There were five or six objects—actually five in a circle with the sixth one in back of it, and they were black, diamond disk-shaped objects . . . They were stationary at one point and then they started moving slowly. We saw them for a total of five seconds, and in one split second, they were ahead of us at least two miles. And we could see them in the distance."

Mario was also impressed with the speed of the objects. "What I saw is four objects shaped like helicopters, exactly like helicopters, but they moved at an incredible, incredible speed. It was like, one minute they were there and in three or four seconds, they were across the horizon, miles and miles away. It's practically impossible for anything that I have ever seen—I've been in the military seven years and I've never seen anything move that rapidly, that fast."

The two men watched the objects hover a few thousand feet above the mountains. They pulled over to get a better look, and the objects darted away, reappearing two miles ahead of them, still in perfect formation. Neither Adam nor Mario were able to identify the objects. As Adam remembered, "They were black aircraft, some kind of craft, and they were very futuristic-looking. They had silverish reflections off the sun, but they were definitely black from what I've seen . . . it was definitely no ordinary aircraft."

Mario's mind kept trying to interpret the objects as something familiar like helicopters, and yet the explanation just didn't fit. "I could have sworn they were helicopters but the only thing is, they didn't have any propellers or whatever you call them. It was oblong and there was a long tail which could be something in the form of a helicopter. And three of the objects were pretty much aligned close to each other and another one was far behind. And I said, 'Adam, what is that, man?' And he looks up and says, 'Damn, I don't know!'"

Both Adam and Mario noticed that the objects moved uniformly, as if they were a single unit. They disagreed, however, on the size and distance of the objects. Mario thought the objects were large and far away while Adam thought the objects were small and close. This type of discrepancy is typical of UFO sightings and actually serves to strengthen the credibility of their report. As any investigator knows, testimonies that match exactly in every detail are unheard of and point toward deception. Normally, testimonies of identical events vary in a number of details.

There is little doubt that these two men saw something strange. Mario does not believe that the objects were conventional aircraft. "I saw like an outline, a metal-black outline. And inside, I couldn't tell you if it was clear or if it was silver, or what . . . all I remember seeing is the oblong oval shape, centered with a big wing, something like a helicopter might have. But if these were military aircraft, they were futuristic-looking . . ."

Adam is equally convinced of the strangeness of their sighting. In fact, immediately following the sighting, they were so excited that they spent the next hour driving up Latigo Canyon and Kanan Dune Road, where they had last seen the objects. They didn't see anything, but they did notice something else that intrigued them. As Adam recalled, "We did come across a couple of people who were just sitting in their lawn chairs along the road. I don't know if this has anything to do with it, but they were just sitting there along the side of the road, parked, just looking up."

UFO watchers? Adam and Mario didn't stop to ask, but continued on their way home. The next day, Adam couldn't get the sighting out of his mind, so he called up the Malibu/Lost Hills Police and asked if there had been any recent reports of UFOs. The officer replied that there had been no recent sightings over Malibu, but that several weeks ago they had received several calls from Topanga Canyon.

Adam briefly reported his sighting and then called up the *Messenger* and reported his sighting to them. Since then, Adam has developed a strong interest in UFOs and has ventured into Topanga in hopes of having another encounter. He has not yet been successful.

Up until now, we have examined only simple sightings. However, because Malibu is a part of the UFO flap area, it is only logical that some of the encounters should be more extensive. The following case is the perfect example.

Robert and his wife lived in Malibu for many years. In late 1992, they moved to Oregon. However, during their residence in Malibu, Robert had experienced an ongoing series of dramatic UFO encounters. What began with simple sightings of strange lights in the sky soon escalated into what appeared to be an object landing in their own backyard!

Their former house is nestled in one of the valleys of Malibu Canyon, off Piuma Road, near the end of a dead-end street. Although the area is isolated, several other houses are in view of their house.

Robert has always had a deep interest in UFOs. His first Malibu sighting was way back in 1975. After meditating one evening, Robert went outside his home and saw a "brilliant orange globe of light floating lazily towards Malibu." There was one other person who also saw the object, which remained in view for about eleven seconds. Robert believes that his meditation may have caused the object to appear because during his meditation, he was vividly imagining what it would be like to see a UFO. He had no idea that he would actually see one.

Robert may have actually started something he wasn't prepared to deal with. A few months later during that same year, Robert had another unusual sighting. He was standing outside his home just before sunset when he saw a "brilliant red ball of light," zipping across the sky at an estimated two-hundred miles per hour. He watched it pass overhead and disappear behind the hills.

Robert didn't have another sighting until 1977. On this occasion, he experienced what he describes as a "two-second sighting of a yellow-orange sphere." As he watched, it moved quickly out of view behind a grove of trees.

Robert had a total of three sightings in Malibu. Then, one evening in October 1978, he had an experience that was much more than just a simple sighting. It was as if his interest in UFOs was being reflected back to him. The tables were turned and now the UFOs were interested in him!

He was alone in the house, resting face down in his bedroom. Suddenly, as if someone had turned on a switch, he felt and heard an intense low vibration. His first impulse was to get up and investigate, but he discovered that he was totally unable to move. As Robert recalled, "I was completely paralyzed and could not even open my eyes until the vibration stopped."

Robert has no idea how long he lay paralyzed or what was causing it. But the moment the vibration stopped, he jumped up and checked the house. Then he went outside and checked around the house. Everything seemed to be in place.

Robert was puzzled and wondered if the experience could possibly have been a dream. Still, he didn't think it was; it was much too real to have been a dream. Then, about two days later, he noticed something very unusual. Right in the center of his own backyard, Robert could clearly see a "lush, vibrant, green seventeen-foot diameter ring of grass about eight inches wide." Examining the area further, Robert noticed that the tip of one of his tall pine trees next to the house was cracked off and hanging down. Also, the grass-ring was directly outside his bedroom sliding door.

Although Robert could only surmise the whole truth, a picture of what happened began to form in his mind. The ring, the broken branch, the paralysis, and the strange buzzing sound all coalesced in his mind into a fantastic conclusion. It was exactly as if a large object had come swooping down out of the sky, clipped off the top of his pine tree, hovered or landed in his backyard, and paralyzed him.

As incredible as this explanation is, Robert feels that it is the only one which fits all the facts. What else could clip off the top of a thirty-foot pine tree? What else could form a perfect eleven-foot circle of lush grass growth? What else could render a person paralyzed and make such a strange buzzing sound?

Robert found the experience hard to believe, but there was no denying the physical evidence. Whenever he felt any doubt, all he had to do was look outside at the strange circle in his backyard. Even after several months, the circle was clearly visible. Finally after about one year, the circle was just barely visible. But then it happened again.

One evening in 1979, Robert was resting face-down on his bed when he suddenly had the distinct feeling of a presence outside his bedroom sliding door. He wanted to get up and see who it was, but then something strange happened. What happened next has all the earmarks of a missing-time abduction.

At the time, Robert wasn't thinking about anything other than what was outside his bedroom door. "I intended to get up and investigate, then woke up some time later and thought nothing more of it until later that week when a second lush, vibrant green seventeen-foot diameter ring of grass appeared on my back lawn, right next to the first one which was still there."

Once he saw the second ring next to the first one, Robert knew that his second experience, a few days earlier, was real. Something had either landed or hovered outside his bedroom. He is aware that he may not consciously remember all of his experience, but as of yet he has not undergone any hypnosis to recall lost memories.

Robert takes an objective stance towards his experience and feels that it was neither positive nor negative. One effect of the experience was to intensify his already deep interest in UFOs.

Two years later, in 1981, Robert had yet another sighting outside his home. He was watching the stars around midnight when he noticed a "faint red light directly overhead which blinked regularly about twice a second."

Robert watched the blinking light for several minutes, but was unable to figure out what it was. The next night, he was surprised to see the same thing. It was obviously not a star, nor did it appear to be a satellite.

On the next night, it was there again. Robert was curious what the blinking light could be. On the fourth night, however, the light did not appear. Robert was never able to come up with a satisfactory explanation.

Then, in 1982, Robert had yet another sighting. He often watched the sky and spotted satellites as they moved in straight lines overhead. That evening, he was watching what he thought was a satellite traveling due east, when it did something that a satellite simply cannot do. Said Robert, "As it passed overhead, it executed a thirty-degree turn to the south, its path forming a perfect angle without any hesitation, continuing on that line until out of sight."

By now Robert was getting used to seeing the objects. He figured that Malibu must be a hotspot. Or maybe the only reason he was seeing so many UFOs was because he was looking for them. He just wasn't sure. All he knew was he kept seeing them.

His next sighting occurred only a few months later. Robert often watched aircraft approach Los Angeles International airport. The planes were easy to recognize because they obeyed a strict flight pattern. One night, however, Robert saw a UFO actually overtake and pass a jet. The sighting began when he saw a "brilliant green light" traveling eastbound on the flight path normally taken by planes. Not only did the light look strange, but it was moving strangely. As Robert watched, the green light quickly caught up to the jet and passed it. He estimated that it was moving three times the speed of the jet. After passing it, the light turned south and followed the coastline until it disappeared over Topanga Canyon. Like most of his sightings, there was complete silence. He viewed the object for a total of twelve seconds.

By now Robert knew that Malibu was a hotspot, so he and his wife decided to attempt to communicate with the objects. On May 12, 1992, they meditated and concentrated on seeing UFOs. The very next night, at 11:00 P.M. they were rewarded with a sighting. As Robert recalled, "We both observed a brilliant incandescent white sphere suddenly appear while descending at a very rapid rate from around five to seven thousand feet. It disappeared below a low ridge-line without slowing. The distance from us was about two to five miles and it was traveling well in excess of the speed of sound, yet it was silent."

Although the sighting lasted mere seconds, both Robert and his wife feel that not only did they see a UFO, but that they actually initiated the encounter using meditation.

A few months after their last sighting, Robert and his wife moved from Malibu. They report that they have not had any sightings at their new home in Oregon.

Probably the closest of all Malibu close encounters were those of Kim Carlsberg, a photographer for the film industry and a former Malibu resident. Kim has had UFO experiences that go far beyond mere sightings. Where most people simply see the objects, Kim has reason to believe that she has been inside them.

Kim has been repeatedly abducted from her Malibu home and has had a number of face-to-face encounters with different types of extraterrestrials. Although her experiences sound incredible, they are corroborated by thousands of other people who have had similar experiences.

Kim has become quite vocal about her abductions. She has spoken publicly at local UFO meetings and has also appeared on the television programs *Sightings* and *The Other Side*. She has been working closely with hypnotherapist and UFO researcher Yvonne Smith, trying to recover and deal with the traumatic memories of her encounters. She has also written a gripping account of her encounters in her book *Beyond My Wildest Dreams*.

Kim related her first Malibu sighting, which occurred late one summer evening in 1988, at her Malibu beachfront home. "As I began to relax, my eyes kept returning to a particularly bright star low on the horizon. Something about it was different. Perhaps it wasn't a star at all. It could have been a sailboat, although it certainly seemed to be above the water, not on it. As I pondered the possibilities, the mystery star shot across the horizon with breathtaking speed and stopped abruptly at Point Dume. I was amazed by its velocity! Palos Verdes, where the light had been hovering, is roughly forty miles south of Point Dume, yet the point of light covered that distance in a matter of seconds . . . What a shame I had to witness such an extraordinary event alone. As though it responded to my thoughts, the brilliant point advanced until it became a luminous sphere some fifty feet in diameter. It ominously hung in the air less than a hundred feet from my window. I couldn't move, I couldn't scream, I couldn't breathe. I didn't know if I was about to see God or the Devil himself. The apparent standoff lasted no more than a minute before the sphere departed as quickly as it appeared. It tore away diagonally through the night sky and vanished."

She also started seeing more objects and actually tried to initiate encounters by sending out telepathic requests. Then one evening in 1991, Kim was awakened by the feeling of "a presence." She stepped outside and saw a light streak across the sky. "Before I could react, a huge, bright, metallic disk magically appeared and hovered inches above the patio fence. I fell to the floor and crawled backwards into the nearest corner. My face flushed and burned, not from fear, but from sheer humiliation at my own reaction. They waited a moment, and I sensed a reassuring message being projected from the craft. We all knew I wasn't ready. The ship disappeared as quickly at it had come. I was so disappointed with myself for losing such an incredible opportunity, but it was still an amazing occurrence. The aliens didn't seem like monsters anymore. Well, not as much. I was deathly afraid of them, and yet, they came at my request. To me that seemed like an act of love. At least, I wanted it to be."

Around this time, Kim began having onboard experiences during which gray-type aliens would come into her bedroom and whisk her away, aboard a UFO. Usually Kim's experiences begin with figures entering her bedroom late at night. As Kim said on the program *Sightings,* "At 4:30 A.M., I saw these four beings just

178

move through this wall like it wasn't there. And they came over to me, two at my feet, two at my head, and they started to lift me up to the ceiling."

Kim also gives a typical description of many peoples' onboard UFO experiences. As she says, "You find yourself on a table and these creatures around you with instruments. And you have no idea what they're going to do and they don't tell you . . . they have a mission, a job to do, and they're doing their job with little respect to their subjects."

Kim says that the extraterrestrials she has seen are of the gray type, which are typically about three or four feet tall, with large dark eyes, over-sized craniums and grayish skin. There's another type of alien, however, that Kim finds extremely frightening. As she says, "There's one being in particular that I always recognize and he's not a gray. He's got bigger eyes. His limbs are very Praying Mantis-like. I remember being on a table with my head turned away and not wanting to look at this. And then when I looked at him, I just recognized him as the one that I hated."

Why are the aliens abducting Kim? According to her, they are taking her ovum and are producing hybrid babies. As Kim explained, "I've been on a table and I've seen something removed from my body that I will call a fetus. The baby was so small I couldn't believe that it could live on its own. I remember putting my finger in the arch of its foot. I was afraid to look at its face. I was afraid to see what it looked like."

As bizarre as Kim's experiences sound, many other people report very similar details. The accounts may differ slightly, but many follow the same basic pattern.

Kim's experiences, like those of many others, often continue with the aliens requesting her to hold the babies and give them love. As Kim recalled, "I've been shown children. I've been shown babies. I've been asked to hold the children and babies. I've been asked to give these children affection. And these children aren't alien children and they're not human children; they're somewhere in-between."

She reports that her encounters have not only been terrifying, but that they have had a profound impact on her life. She has trouble with relationships because her boyfriends would often end up having terrifying encounters. Usually, she said, whoever she's with is put to sleep and she is the only one taken. However, sometimes the experiences do involve the person who just happens to be with her at the time.

One of the most incredible aspects of Kim's encounters is her declaration that she was taken into what appeared to be a large human-made underground base where she saw aliens and humans working together. She does not know where the base is located or why she was taken there. She is very careful to report the facts as she knows them.

Kim is very clear that she does not enjoy being abducted and says that the terror is almost unimaginable. She said that the aliens have caused physical damage to her body. If she had it her way, she would prefer that the experiences would simply end.

She recently moved away from Malibu, but her experiences are still continuing. In April 1993, she had another bedroom visitation. Her current relationship was going well and she absolutely did not want her boyfriend to have an experience. So when the aliens showed up in her bedroom, she felt herself becoming extremely angry, and before she knew it, she gathered all her strength and shouted out, "No!"

To her surprise, the aliens left. It was one of the first times she has ever successfully stopped an abduction.

Although Kim's story is bizarre, it is supported by hundreds of other people across the world who have had similar experiences. There is little doubt among researchers that onboard UFO experiences take place. The emphasis is shifting from trying to prove these experiences to learning how to deal with them. Today Kim describes herself as "a vegetarian, an animal rights activist, and an impassioned environmentalist." She also says that as a result of her encounters, she is a "hands-on healer" and is learning channeling. Interestingly, many abductees fit the same pattern. Whether this is a result of the encounters or perhaps the reason for them, remains a matter of speculation. Whatever the case, there seems to be much to learn and gain from these types of experiences.

Malibu, like Topanga Canyon, is a hotspot. The encounters are highly reminiscent of the Topanga encounters and are obviously closely related. As numerous as the Malibu sightings are, they are still rivaled by those of Topanga Canyon, which remains the focus for most of the encounters.

15

The Northridge Quake Encounters

ON JUNE 14, 1992, literally hundreds of unidentified flying objects were seen by various residents over Topanga Canyon. Two years later, a similar event occurred involving more than a dozen UFOs seen by multiple witnesses. It was the day before the Northridge, California earthquake—which registered 6.8 on the Richter scale—when one Topanga Canyon resident first noticed something strange.

Marcellina was a resident of the trailer park located at the Top o' Topanga. She had lived there for several years with her boyfriend, Lewis. She had no idea that she was about to experience a UFO adventure that would leave her totally transformed.

The experience actually began with a series of bizarre events that may or may not be related. First, Marcellina woke up the morning before the earthquake with a changed attitude. Normally she is very giving and trusting. She dislikes confronting people who harm her. However, on this day, she was unaccountably seized with a strange impulse to change. As she recalled, "It was the day before the earthquake, and all of a sudden I had a different attitude towards the people I knew and them basically screwing me over all the time. And I started telling them how I felt. It was very hard for me usually to ever tell anyone, 'I don't like the way you are treating me,' or whatever I felt. I could never do that. That day, I could not stop."

Later on that day, Marcellina and Lewis drove into the San Fernando Valley in their Mustang convertible. As they were passing a gas station, Marcellina heard herself blurt out, "Gasoline! Fire!" She had no reason to say this. Her boyfriend pulled over and started searching the backseat for a lit cigarette. Marcellina asked him what he was doing.

"You just screamed out 'fire!'" he explained.

Marcellina told him that she had no idea why she said that. He looked at her and just shook his head and continued driving. They went to a friend's house where Marcellina was suddenly overcome with a strange "knowing sensation." She somehow knew exactly what their friend was going to say. Marcellina recounted, "I whispered to Lewis what I predicted he wanted to eat, and then he came out and said the same exact thing I predicted which was another weird thing that day."

They then went to a local New Age bookstore and bought several crystals. As they were driving back, Marcellina had the impulse to look up in the sky where she saw something very unusual. "All of a sudden I looked up in the sky and I had seen something that looked like it kind of exploded in the sky . . . almost . . . like it was fireworks. I tried to get Lewis to look, but he was turning so he couldn't see. . . . This was about 9:00 P.M. It was like someone set off big fireworks or firecrackers or whatever. But it didn't make a sound or anything. . . .Well after that, I kept looking in the sky."

As they headed back through the valley, Marcellina noticed that the traffic on the streets was unusually light, which she thought was strange considering the next day was the Martin Luther King, Jr. holiday and many people didn't have to work. Shortly after, another minor strange event happened. Marcellina recalled it. "As we were driving back towards Topanga, right near the gas station, fire trucks started going by, right where I said, 'Fire! Gasoline!' And I said, 'Oh, that's just a coincidence.'"

It was not to be the last strange event to occur that evening. Marcellina and Lewis then drove to the Spiral Staircase, a New Age bookstore at the junction of Topanga Canyon Boulevard and Old Topanga Canyon Road, in the heart of Topanga Canyon. Marcellina again felt the impulse to buy more crystals. There they saw something else which made them both reconsider the day's events. Marcellina recalled, "I started looking up in the sky, and I started seeing what kind of looks like the bottom of a blimp, and lights flickering. There was yellow, purple, red and they kept on flickering, like changing from yellow, red, purple; yellow, red, purple. I kept looking and I kept seeing more. And they were crossing over Topanga. And I said, 'Lewis, what the hell are those things?'

"He said, 'They're planes.'

"I said, 'Those are not planes. Planes just don't fly over Topanga that way.'

"And more and more, they kept on going. And they were in sync the way they were going. And Lewis all of a sudden started getting the creeps.

He said, 'Let's go back. It's cold!'

"And I said, 'It's not cold. I'm burning up.' So we headed back up towards the Top o' Topanga again and I kept on looking at these things all through the sky. They were probably about a hundred feet up. They were low. That's why I knew they weren't planes. You know what they looked like? They looked like trams. It had the same type of thing where one was going, the other was going, and it was all [in sync]. And I just kept on thinking it was pretty weird. It wasn't the speed of a plane. It was slower. They were . . . following each other."

Marcellina stared at the lights in fascination. The colors were vivid, and the objects looked solid. She had no idea what the objects could be. As they drove, she counted at least fifty of the strange craft moving in a row across the ridgetops. By this time, they had reached the bookstore. They jumped out and stood near the creek watching the lights. Marcellina kept on hoping another car would come by so she could flag them down and show them the lights, but it was as if the roads were deserted. Marcellina went into the Spiral Staircase and bought some more crystals then returned outside.

Lewis said, "Let's go home. I'm cold."

Marcellina agreed. They got in the car and began the short return trip. It was almost 10:00 P.M. at this point. Almost immediately, Marcellina noticed more of the strange objects in the sky. "There was like a bunch of them. I was thinking maybe it could have been something—like they were setting off one of those Air Force things, and they were just testing something. But they didn't look like they were planes."

In a few minutes, they were at the entrance to their trailer park. Near their trailer park on the ridgetop directly west, there are two large water towers. It was then that events took an even more bizarre turn. Marcellina said, "Lewis was driving my car into the card-key place for the mobile home. And I said, 'No, no, reverse the car. Let me put the card-key in.' He's looking at me like, why do you want to do that? I said, 'Shut up, just do it.'

"So he reverses the car, and I'm putting the card-key in, and as I look across the road over the water tower, this huge humongous gigantic red object, lit up red, little lights—it came flying over the water tower. It was so big, I thought they were maybe filming a movie. There are two water towers up there and I would say it was about three or four times the width of those water towers. The thing was huge. It was very big. And it started heading towards us. Lewis was freaking out. I mean, he was almost like paralyzed. He wanted to get away. And I kept saying, 'No, don't move. I want to see what it is.'

"It was shaped like a crystal, like a rectangular-shaped thing, but it was pointed at the front. The whole thing had red lights flickering, but I can tell you this much, it was see-through. I could see the stars through it. So, to me, you know at first I thought it was a big kite. And then I thought, could it be they're doing a movie? Then I thought, could it be a UFO? I didn't know what to really think, but in my mind I knew it was a UFO. But like I said, I wasn't afraid either. So in the middle of this thing was like a little round thing. I think it was white, but it had a yellow, purple and red light in the middle of it, and that was the only part that wasn't see-through. Behind it, it was trailing another unit. It was almost like a little buggy. It was attached by red lights. Now I could almost think that all those things I saw flying would fit into this thing. And it went right over our heads and hovered. Lewis didn't remember the humming. I told Lewis, 'Hurry up! Turn around! Let's go follow where it's going!' All of a sudden, it disappeared. It was kind of hard to even try and follow because if we followed it, we would have to go off the cliffs of Topanga. So it had disappeared."

Marcellina ran inside and called a girlfriend who lived directly east of Topanga Canyon and told her to look for the object. Her friend did as instructed and returned to the phone with the announcement that it was too foggy to see anything. Marcellina insisted that there was a UFO outside, but her friend said that the weather made it impossible to see anything. Marcellina called another friend in the San Fernando Valley who also said that the fog was too thick to see anything. Marcellina went outside and looked up. In Topanga Canyon, the weather was still perfectly clear.

Lewis stayed in the house, trying to deal with what they had just seen. It wasn't long before Marcellina saw more objects. "Lewis had run into the house, freaked out. I could not go into the house. I wanted to stay outside. And as I was . . . outside, from the valley side . . . all of a sudden, big white beams of light were flying over Topanga. And then they would disappear. They weren't from the street. They were from the sky. And it was almost like big searchlights. And I heard hovering sounds with that too. It would like come right up to our park, and then it would disappear. So I just kept on staying outside. Then they started whining; they kept coming out trying to get me back in. My neighbor next door had finally come out. I said, 'Oh, my God! Michael, you won't believe what I've seen tonight! I saw a UFO!'

"He said, 'What were *you* on?'

"I said, 'Listen, I saw a UFO.' We looked up into the sky and the sky was very clear. But there was a lot of electricity going on in the air."

Marcellina told her neighbor that something unusual was happening. He returned inside while Marcellina stayed outside. Not only did she continue to see unusual light activity, but it felt as if the atmosphere itself was crackling with energy. After a few hours, Marcellina finally went inside. Both of them were so excited by the night's ordeal, they decided to sleep in the living room. A few hours later, the Northridge earthquake struck.

Topanga Canyon is only about ten miles away from the epicenter of the quake. The instant it hit, several homes throughout the canyon were thrown off their foundations, the roads buckled and cracked, huge crevasses opened up along the ridgetops, landslides roared down the steep canyon walls. In the trailer park at the Top o' Topanga, it was chaos. The quake threw several of the trailers into the air, destroying them. It ruptured gas lines, and a few of the trailers in the park exploded in towering flames.

Marcellina's home was devastated. Nearly every material object she owned was destroyed. Thankfully, neither she nor her boyfriend were hurt. However, when Marcellina surveyed her bedroom, she was shocked to discover that had she been in her bed, she would have been killed by a large buffalo-head sculpture that had stood next to her bed but was now lying on the bed, exactly where she would have been sleeping.

Once the tremors finally stopped, Marcellina crawled outside and saw the other trailers burning. She suddenly remembered her earlier premonition, when she blurted out, "Gasoline! Fire!" Now, here she was in the middle of a fire caused by a gas-leak.

Finally, the fire department arrived. Because the water mains were also ruptured, they rushed up to the water tanks which were supposed to be filled with water for just such an emergency, but the tanks were empty. This detail shocked Marcellina because she had seen the objects hovering over the water tanks hours earlier. It would be nearly a month before the gas and water mains were repaired.

But it was the earthquake–UFO connection that most impressed Marcellina. Were the UFOs warning her of the quake? Could they somehow be responsible for it? Marcellina recalled, "I was totally freaked out. I kept on trying to call the news to find out if anything had happened. I tried calling Griffith Park Observatory to find out. I kept on trying to call everybody possible because of the relationship of what I saw and then the earthquake five hours later . . . I mean, this was something I could not get out of my mind. Everyone I spoke to, I told [them] the story. They all thought I was nuts."

The next day, Marcellina talked to her neighbor Michael. They both checked to make sure each other was all right, and then Michael apologized for disbelieving Marcellina's story. He said, "I believe you now."

Later that day, Marcellina was sitting poolside, recovering from the shock of losing all her possessions. To her surprise, she was reacting uncharacteristically optimistic. She sat next to another Topanga resident. They began talking about the earthquake. Marcellina said, "I was kind of having a good time even though everything I owned [was broken]. I was sitting there talking to this girl, I had never met her in my life before, but she had lived up there. And in talking, she was a little bit nervous, and I was a little bit nervous. I finally broke down. I said, 'Believe it or not, I think this earthquake was caused by a UFO.'

"She said, 'Why do you say that?'

"I said, 'Last night I saw a lot of weird activity in the sky.'

"She said, 'I was on Sherman Way last night when I saw a lot of weird stuff in the sky. It almost looked like there was video games going on.'

"I looked at her and said, 'That's exactly what I saw.' And the friend's house that she was at, everyone wanted to go in the house and she [wanted] to go outside to sit and watch. Now she didn't see the UFO, but what she did see were those big white lights. So she was one other person who did see something."

Later I received independent confirmation of Marcellina's sighting. On the night before the earthquake, a group of men reported seeing "very unusual activity in the sky." Although the witnesses haven't been interviewed, they had no contact with Marcellina and had no idea that there were other witnesses. The men were friends of a woman who was soon to become yet another Topanga Canyon UFO eyewitness.

A few days after the earthquake, Marcellina went to the local FEMA office for assistance. There she experienced another remarkable coincidence. "There was this man I met after the earthquake through FEMA. He was a Native American. I was sitting at the FEMA office and he said, 'Why are you so shaky?'

"I said, 'Oh, you wouldn't even believe.' I wasn't afraid to tell anyone of this because these people were so afraid of what happened with the earthquake that, to me, it was almost funny for me to tell them: 'Oh, yeah, it happened because of the UFO and I knew it was going to happen the night before.' I mean, I didn't know exactly it was going to be an earthquake, but I knew it was going to be something.

"And when I was talking to this man, he said, 'Go ahead, tell me. We're here to help.'

"I said, 'We're here to help? If you want to try to help on this one, you're welcome to.' And I told him the story. And it just so happens, this man had seen the same exact description of what I had seen a couple of years before up in the hills somewhere. He drew it exactly the way I drew it out. He remembers being able to see the stars through the thing. He said that he became very psychic and intuitive and spiritual after that."

Marcellina had begun to notice a transformation in herself. Not only was she less materialistic, but there were other changes. One was that she felt compelled to make a series of paintings portraying landscapes of alien-looking planets and outer-space scenes.

But events still seemed to be in progress. It was about two weeks after the earthquake that Marcellina experienced an alien visitation directly in her home. She was sitting in her living room looking outside when she suddenly saw the image of figure coalescing in front of her. She couldn't believe what she was seeing; however, she noticed instantly that the figure was decidedly strange. "It kind of looked like it was a cat face without any hair, and a combination of a skeleton face. It was almost like a holographic type of thing."

She sat there, stunned by the image, trying to determine exactly what was happening, when the phone rang. Lewis answered the phone from the other room and buzzed Marcellina with the intercom. Marcellina picked up the phone but couldn't hear anybody on the line. She hung up the phone and looked back at the image. She slowly began to realize how strange the experience actually was. The intercom rang again and Lewis said, "What's wrong with you? Frank is on the phone."

Marcellina said, "Tell Frank I'll call him back. Get out here right now!"

Marcellina couldn't believe what she was seeing and she desperately wanted another witness. "I was hoping he was coming to see what I was seeing. And he wasn't coming out. So I kept on calling his name and he was still not coming out. So I tried getting up to go call him and my legs would not move. After a little while, I actually had an orgasm, just sitting on the couch. The weird part was, while I was sitting there looking at this thing, I was trying to write down things it was telling me. And it was telling me that they were trying to invent ways of intercourse. They needed babies. They were just telling me a bunch of things telepathically. There would be more earthquakes. And then you know, we had all those earthquakes all over the world . . . I had changed my living room after the earthquake with a whole bunch of pictures I had painted of planets. And they told me that's not exactly the way it looked there. It was more of inside a planet, crystallized. It was like crystals where they were coming from . . . When I saw the vision, the thing that I wrote down was that I would be able to heal myself and I would be able to heal people. If they wanted me to heal them, I would be able to heal them."

After an undetermined time, the vision left and Marcellina was able to move. She rushed to her boyfriend and told him what happened. He didn't know what to make of her story, but was very supportive. Marcellina knew that her experience was real. A few weeks later, she received powerful evidence that the experience had affected her not only mentally and emotionally, but physically. She discovered she was pregnant. Circumstances placed her in the position to test her talents to physically heal herself, just as the figure with the cat-like eyes had told her. As she recalled, "A few weeks later [after the living room visitation], I all of a sudden had this bulge in the left side of my stomach. And I had gone to the doctor. I went to the emergency room and they wanted to do surgery. They said, 'You know, maybe it could be a hernia, or we're not really sure what it is.'

"I didn't want to have an operation, and I decided in my head, this is going to go away. And it went away three days later. Three days after that, I dropped a seventy-five pound slate of marble on my foot. It didn't cut my foot, but you could see where there was an indentation in my foot, probably being broken. Two days later, it went away. Then, about four months later, I had a miscarriage and there was nothing in the sac."

Marcellina was stunned by the turn of events. She knew something very profound had happened to her and she longed to share it with some one who would understand. The experience with the cat-like figure also sparked a curious memory from her childhood. She suddenly remembered having seen the figure before, when she was just a little girl.

As a young child, Marcellina had looked at the French doors in her parents' living room when she saw a short figure staring at her. "There was this thing standing at my parents' French doors. Its face was like a whitish face. The way my mind made it look was . . . almost like a clown-type face. It had black eyes. I wasn't afraid, but I was always confused to know if I was dreaming or not. I basically was convinced I really saw this thing. And it wasn't like a type of thing where it was a person. I know that started when I was young. What I remember was, there was a bush with orange flowers. What I did was I made it look like a clown because of the orange flowers near the head. So I always had a fear of clowns since that time. Because it was like someone looking in my window. And why is this person dressed like a clown? But it wasn't really a clown. When I think back now, it was not a clown. But I was always afraid of clowns after that. Like I said, when I really think back on a lot of the stories and things that happened to me when I was a kid, like that thing I imagined was a clown at my window, I know I was awake. And me making the flowers turn into something that looked like a wig, it was exactly as if it was a cat face without hair with very big eyes."

Interestingly, UFO researcher Budd Hopkins reports that he has several cases of abductees who have this same bizarre phobia—fear of clowns. As Hopkins writes in *Witnessed,* "I have encountered at least five abductees with this same dread fear of clowns, in every case dating from childhood. Most cite clowns' scary, exaggerated eyes and the mask-like painted faces. It would seem that for some abductees, seeing the natural human physical body and/or face stylized or distorted triggers memories of the aliens' non-human appearance."[2]

It was obvious to Marcellina that the figure she saw as a child and the figure she saw a few weeks after the earthquake were one and the same. She gives the typical description of a short figure with a large head, large wrap-around black eyes, short height, whitish skin.

Marcellina also remembered that there had been many occasions during which she had seen strange lights near her home. Somehow they always seemed to elude her. "I have seen things in the canyons. Then when I take my car to go look to see what it was, it would be gone. So whoever was with me at the time would think I was just nuts, you know, like chasing rainbows that weren't there. But I knew I was really seeing something."

After the latest encounter, Marcellina's transformation accelerated. "After all that happened, losing a lot of materialistic stuff, (once meaning a lot to me), all of a sudden things that were important to me were rocks and nature stuff. It's changed my life, I think, to a positive way."

Marcellina now has an obsessive interest in UFOs. Shortly after her encounter, she sought information and was finally put in touch with Los Angeles-based UFO investigator Don Waldrop. He investigated her account and, satisfied with the legitimacy of the case, arranged a hypnotic regression for Marcellina. For some reason, however, the session failed. Marcellina was puzzled because she felt no fear and was eager to explore the experience. She speculated that perhaps there was nothing more to remember. She was fully conscious during her experience and remembered it vividly.

Marcellina also noticed a marked increase in her intuitive abilities. One incident involved a premonition of the collision between Jupiter and comet Shoemaker-Levy. Ultimately, the experience changed Marcellina physically, mentally and spiritually. In each way, the final result was positive. Today, Marcellina is eager to expand her knowledge about UFOs and spread the word of her own experience.

Her experience has many remarkable parallels to other cases in Topanga. She is not the only witness to report seeing dozens upon dozens of objects. She is not the only witness to report a transparent object. Nor is she the only person to report short telepathic beings who give predictions about earthquakes and perform healings. Nor is this the only case in which the UFOs show an intense interest in human reproduction. Even the buzzing noise, the strange shape of the craft, the odd searchlight-like beams are all part of the mysterious puzzle of events that continue to occur over Topanga Canyon. Marcellina's case is obviously highly complex and cannot be easily defined or categorized. She knows in her heart that she had a real experience that left her permanently transformed.

Unknown to her, many other people were about to see a similar or perhaps even the same object she had seen. In fact, 1994 would prove to be quite busy indeed. The Topanga UFO wave was still underway.

16

More Topanga Encounters

THE UFO WAVE that began in 1992 was still going strong in 1994. For whatever reason, the objects just kept coming. That year provided a treasure trove of new reports. Some reports involved unexplained lights; some involved metallic ships. At least one report involved an apparent abduction. Interestingly, the majority of the reports that year were centered around the Top o' Topanga.

The first report involved the case of Marcellina, which we have already explored. I asked Don Waldrop to confirm some of the details of Marcellina's story. He graciously sent the following response:

January 16, 1994
The night before the Northridge earthquake, Marcellina and her roommate, Lewis, were coming back home to Top o' Topanga about 9:30 P.M. Because she had the card-key and he was driving, she asked Lewis to back up so she could insert the card into the electronic gate lock. While facing

down the driveway (northwest), they saw—coming toward them from over the water tanks on the other side of Topanga Boulevard—a large transparent flying object.

It was rectangular with the front end coming to a point—[Marcella] called it crystal-shaped. It had many red moving lights and there was a cluster of red, yellow, and green lights in the bottom center. It looked as if it was towing another smaller structure in the shape of a half circle that was also lit with the red lights.

The craft slowly passed over them at an extremely low altitude, heading east-southeast, and disappeared approximately 500 to 1000 feet away. The red lights were small, like Christmas tree lights, and were moving in sequence from front to back. She felt she could see stars through the objects.

There are many further issues related to this story that are being investigated, including other sightings, possible abductions, and healings.

Marcellina's case has been thoroughly investigated. She has been interviewed multiple times by different investigators and continues to tell the same incredible story. Not only does she have witnesses to support her story, there is also the physical evidence in the form of unexplained healings. Perhaps the most incredible aspect is that Marcellina is only one of many people in Topanga Canyon and across the world who are having this type of experience.

Marcellina was impressed by the odd crystal shape of the object. As it would turn out, many other witnesses were to spot objects in the same area in the following months, and virtually all of them would describe the object as having the same unusual shape.

Less than one month after Marcellina's encounter, another Topanga resident discovered that Topanga is a UFO hotspot. She had her encounter in early February, while driving to her home up Entrada. She had just recently moved into Topanga and had no idea that there were regular sightings in the canyon. A few months after her sighting, she saw my flyer and called me. She reluctantly agreed to an interview but insisted on remaining completely anonymous. She was very guarded and obviously didn't want any publicity. She admitted she was actually calling from a pay phone, and only after we had talked for several minutes would she even share her first name. We will call this woman Samantha. Here is her account:

"I was driving home at around midnight up Entrada Road along Muerdago. There's one place that has a curve, a panorama, a really good view of the sky. And I just stopped my car and looked up and I saw a red light. And it was pretty far up, but it was just floating and bobbing up and down. And then it started—it would disappear and then there would be a red thing and it would reappear. It was like it was coming in and out of dimensions, into this dimension. And then it would cross really fast, and I would just see this stream of light where it would cross. And it would appear again. And I would see it just kind of bouncing and blinking, and kind of appearing and disappearing. The main thing that just blew me away was how it could move that way. So it was pretty interesting. I knew that a plane couldn't move that way . . . it was moving really fast. It was like hopping, appearing and disappearing, and then reappearing. It was really beautiful to watch.

"I didn't see it turning. It moved in straight lines and it was making patterns, like I could see almost because it was moving so fast that I would see streams of it. It looked like it was almost drawing. I could see streams from the way it was moving. I would think, 'Oh, my God! What was that?!' It looked like something from geometry or something. The streams were sometimes shapes.

"I've seen a UFO before, not here. So it didn't surprise me so much to see one. But it did surprise me to see the way it moved. Because I've only seen one before. That was very different looking. This one, it just challenged my whole thinking that something could move that way. It was just mind-boggling. It didn't scare me."

After talking more with Samantha, she hinted that this encounter or perhaps others might have been more extensive than she originally revealed. "I wouldn't be surprised if I have more—if I've been abducted, and I've been suppressing it. I wouldn't be surprised if I've had any other experiences since I've been here. I just haven't done regression to find out. I have memories of it. Vague memories."

In March 1994, still another anonymous Topanga resident called me to report his encounters. In fact, he reports that on several evenings as he drove through Topanga, he sighted strange objects hovering near the Top o' Topanga area.

The resident, whom we shall call Taylor, had called me earlier to report a sighting but declined to be formally interviewed. On this occasion, he cautiously agreed, mainly because he was planning to move out of the canyon in about one month. He had only moved into Topanga Canyon a few months earlier. Before that, Taylor's friend gave him an ominous warning about Topanga. As Taylor recalled, "My friend knows something, but I can't say. He said, 'Did you see UFOs up there?' I said, 'No.' He said, 'Well, tell me when you do or if you do.' That's when I was moving up here, because I hadn't been living here that long. He probably knows something."

Evidently, Taylor's friend knew what he was talking about. Shortly after Taylor moved into the canyon, he began seeing objects, not once or twice, but practically every night for weeks on end. Taylor's testimony follows:

"This thing was like a jet, but it had different lights. It looked like it had wings, but it was going too slow. It was way up in the sky. It was going somewhere, cruising, and it turned. It did an arc. It was just going really slow. I think there was another one before it, because it had like ten escorts flying, just buzzing around . . . little ones. They were flying around every night, just the escorts. They were like helicopters, but they were silent. You would think you'd hear them if they were flying by. They fly down by where the store is. To me that's how far down they looked. Because I live up a ways, towards the top . . . But they came over my house too. They just flew. They went right up the ridge, the escorts did. The big ones, they're more out

on the other side of the road . . . they looked like helicopters but they didn't make any noise. And there
were so many of them, and every night they were flying. I just didn't want to say anything about them."

Taylor was confused by the uncanny resemblance of
the smaller objects to helicopters, especially because it
was obvious to him that they were not helicopters. He
is certain the larger object was not a plane, because on
one occasion, it approached his car quite close, and he
was actually able to hear the object. He gives a typical
description of the sound of a UFO. "I did hear the big
one once, because that was like the second time. I did
see it two times. And one time I didn't hear any noise.
But one time I heard like a humming sound, like *mmm-
mmm* . . . that's what it sounded like. When I saw this,
I thought, 'Wow! There must be a lot of people seeing
this!' They were going down there, by the ocean. One
night they were up at the Top o' Topanga flying, right
there where the hill comes up and it goes over. That's
where they were. They were even with the road then,
almost. They were coming down low."

It was the way the object looked and moved that
most impressed Taylor. Again he gives a description
corroborated by other reports that had not yet been
reported. "It was moving like it was just lifting, like it
was just hovering. But it was moving. It had some
speed, but not much . . . It was so big that you'd think
it would have to have more speed to get enough lift. It
just kind of cruised. It went by and it was gone. I was
getting all scared when I was watching it. It was weird-
looking. It was strange whatever it was. It would have
been like a disk that's not really round. It looked like

some kind of flat thing, but it was long. To me, it looked like a bus, but flatter, not really tall . . . like if you were close, it would be really wide—like a type of rectangle or something."

The flyer I posted throughout Topanga showed a typical saucer-shaped object. Most of the Topanga residents say the objects have a much stranger shape. Taylor, like most eyewitnesses, struggled to find words to convey an accurate description. "Yeah, it was strange whatever it was. It's not round like you have on this picture. You have a picture of it, and it's not round. It isn't like that. That's more like science fiction. This thing, it looks like—it's hard . . . it's just lights. Mostly it's just lights. I couldn't see anything on it. It had colored lights on it too."

Taylor pointed out the smaller objects to his wife, and they watched them together for several hours. "They stayed. I don't know if that thing turned, if it went over the mountain and it was on the other side and I couldn't see it, if it was still there or what. They were still flying around for hours. Even the next night they were flying around. They were flying around, but I didn't see the big one. They flew around all night."

Taylor is certain that he saw something other than a plane. "Jets don't come up through the canyon, not that low. It was just going right up through the middle of the canyon. There's a ravine between the mountains, and it was going through there, at the top of the mountains. It was above me, but it was below the mountain tops. It was in the canyon."

Taylor said that he has seen the objects several times. "Just driving in and out, I've seen them every night for like a week. I haven't seen them for the last two weeks, but I've seen them for like a month straight. I've seen them every evening. I believe they're from another planet. I believe there's other people coming here, other space people. I was going to get my friend's video camera, but I haven't seen them. I used to see them every night. I'd say, 'Man, this place is invaded!' Every night for like two weeks. And I didn't think they would leave because they kept coming. Most of the time I'd see like three of them circling around. Why are they always circling? Do I think they're UFOs? Yes, I think they're UFOs. I have no doubt that they'll come back."

This next sighting is significant, as I can personally vouch for the witness because on this occasion, I had the wonderful good fortune to join the ranks of Topanga Canyon UFO eyewitnesses. Actually it wasn't exactly luck. I had carefully studied the reports and determined when and where in Topanga was the prime location to have a UFO encounter. I had seen some strange things in Topanga before, but the next sighting was the strangest.

On the evening of July 16, 1994, just a few weeks after the television program *Encounters* had ventured into Topanga with CSETI and successfully initiated an encounter with an anomalous light, we returned to Topanga State Park. It was my first time functioning as leader of the Los Angeles Chapter of CSETI. There were seven of us altogether. As our location, we had chosen a site very near to the site used by *Encounters*, only more remote. Still, it was in the heart of Topanga State Park, where the majority of objects have been seen. On this particular evening, there were other CSETI groups across the United States doing live fieldwork. It was kind of an experiment with simultaneous fieldwork.

We all settled into our site and sat in a circle. It was about 10:00 P.M. and we all sat with our eyes closed in meditation. About halfway through the meditation, I suddenly had a strong impulse to open my eyes and look up. This is not something I have ever done because doing so disturbs your relaxation. However, the impulse was so strong that I just looked straight up. I was staring straight up, thinking, "Okay, you're out there, now show yourselves!" Literally, as if on cue, I saw a light appear precisely where I was looking. At first it was just a little pinprick of light, but in a split second, it had grown in brightness to being much brighter than the brightest star in the sky. It remained motionless, except that it expanded in size and brightness. The light had a very milky quality and was very bright. I had no time to think that this might be a shooting star because within two or three seconds, the light had expanded to the size of a full moon. It kept getting bigger. If the sky was a big glass table and you were under it looking up, it looked like somebody was pouring milk over the surface. The circle expanded until it covered a huge area of the sky, well beyond the size of five full moons. I had never seen anything like this. It continued to expand filling most of the sky. And then, instantly, it winked out. I was stunned.

The whole sighting had lasted no longer than five seconds, but I was completely convinced I had seen something unusual. I knew that it wasn't a shooting star, fireball, plane or anything like that. If anyone else had seen it, they would have known. I looked around at everyone else, but they all still had their eyes closed. The light was already gone so I didn't tell anyone what I had seen until the meditation was over. In a weird way, I felt like I was meant to see it. Nobody else saw anything. Still, I knew that I had seen something unusual. The fact that I opened my eyes and looked up right before I saw them also makes me wonder if they were perhaps impressing me to look up. I remember actually thinking they were up there, and that they were about to show themselves. I had opened my eyes for only a few seconds before the light appeared.

I later found out that CSETI groups in Arizona and Colorado both reported similar encounters. The experiment was a success. Further stunning confirmation of the sighting came about a month later when I got a call from two people who were driving through the canyon on the exact same evening. In fact, at what may have been the exact same time, they both saw an object flying over the ridge, no more than two miles from where our CSETI group sat!

At around 9:00 or 10:00 P.M., Topanga resident Reina Massey, and her boyfriend, Bruce Merrifield, drove south into the canyon when they saw a large object hovering over the Top o' Topanga area.

Bruce was the first to notice it. "We were driving down the road and I turned around and I looked, and I saw this thing with a bunch of bright lights. All of a sudden, it was appearing over the side of a hill. And then, all of a sudden, it just stopped. Then it just pitched itself sideways and all I saw was the bottom of it . . . it was kind of strange. It was only like a hundred feet above the ground and it didn't have any noise. There was no noise whatsoever. And we have a convertible and the top was down, so we would hear it. It was really bizarre . . . it was huge. And it had a weird shape to it. It was like the roof of a house, but it tapered to the bottom. So it was skinnier at the bottom . . . bigger at the top. It had five sides to it. It was huge. When I first saw it, it had like sixteen lights on the bottom. And then as I turned around to figure out what it was, they quadrupled in number."

Bruce stared intently at the object, carefully observing its features. He noticed there was one large light on the bottom center of the craft, and several other little lights spaced around the perimeter. He was most impressed by the huge size and unusual shape of the craft. "I don't know how to describe it. If you look at a barn, if you look at it from the side, how it goes up, joins the roof and makes a triangle, goes straight down and hits the bottom. It was tapered so it was flat. I know for sure it was pretty flat. It was solid. It was absolutely solid. And it was a strange-looking metal material. There were no wings. I didn't see any kind of hydraulics on it at all."

Bruce got such a good look at the craft, that he was able to conclude to his satisfaction that the object could not be a plane. In fact, the craft seemed to be aware of them—it had stopped and actually seemed to pose for them. Bruce recalled, "When we saw it, it stopped. It just stopped cold where it was. Then it went flat. Then it just turned up and all we saw was just the bottom. And it just stopped there for like fifteen or twenty seconds . . . I would have known for sure if it was a plane. That's something I would have known. In fact, I was really skeptical about it. It really intrigued me because there was no noise. There was absolutely no noise. For something being that low, you'd hear it. If it was a jet, for sure you would hear it. If it was a 747 or something like that, you would hear it too . . . it was right above it, the peak there, I mean like right above it, within like ten or twenty feet above it. I mean, it was low. I had a bird's eye view of the whole thing. It was just incredible. It was too low to be an airplane. It was just too low to be an airplane because they would be endangering houses in that area. It had absolutely no shape to anything as far as an airplane, a jet, or even a passenger plane."

As he sat there watching the object, Bruce never felt any fear. He said, "Not really scared, more or less it really intrigued me more than anything else. I was curious, but my girlfriend was scared. It was quite an amazing experience. It was something that I never thought I would see."

Reina Massey reports the same details. "It just turned on its side and we saw the bottom part. It was facing us, the bottom. It was like tilted. I didn't really watch it because I was driving. I just kept turning around my head, and we stopped. Bruce noticed it. He said, 'What's that?' I'm all, 'Oh, nothing.' I didn't really look. And then I started looking because it was so big, and we were getting close to it. And I'm like, 'Wow! I don't know what it is!' I kept looking over at it, and it was just so odd. I've never seen anything looking like that. He pointed it out to me. It was really big, and it was like a triangle shape—not really a triangle shape, maybe an octagon . . . it was very unusual. I don't know if it was a spaceship, but what could it have been? This one wasn't round as everyone says it should be. It was like a flying boat."

Reina also noticed the strange lights on the craft, some of which were colored. "There were red ones. I didn't really look too closely at the lights. I wasn't really focusing on the lights. I just saw the whole thing. There was like red and yellow. That's what I remember. No green or blue. There was a lot. First there was just a few. Then I think it turned on its side or something, and there was a lot more on the bottom. I wish we had a camera or something. That would have been so awesome."

Reina had slowed the car down but didn't actually stop. As they drove by the object, they looked at each other and realized that they were seeing an actual UFO. Reina quickly maneuvered a U-turn and returned to where the object had been hovering. They got there just in time to watch it glide away very quickly. Bruce said, "It dropped down and took off, I'd have to say east. That's exactly what happened. It was truly bizarre . . . we stopped and turned around and tried to find it again. But it was gone. And we drove back to look over the valley to see if there was anything in the air at the time, and there was nothing around."

Reina also remembers searching for the object, hoping to catch another glimpse. "We didn't even realize what it was until we went down the road a little bit—after we couldn't find it, looking for it again. Bruce said, 'That was a spaceship!' I'm like, 'No way! There's no way that could have been a spaceship!' He said, 'Think about it, Reina. What else could it have been?' I told my mom about it because she's really into that stuff, and she said, 'I don't know, it doesn't sound like a blimp or anything.' Because that's the only other thing we thought that could be that low . . . I kind of didn't want to believe that it was a spaceship, because it's kind of strange. But I do."

Reina said that the close-up sighting of the UFO caused her fear to battle with her excitement. "Yeah, it did a little bit, after I started thinking about it. I've heard about people being sucked up. You know the stories. But I was very happy. I've never seen anything like that. I've always wanted to. I wasn't sucked up or anything. But I did see it, and it was really neat."

Bruce's father happens to be an airplane designer and Bruce often assists him in his work. Because of this, Bruce is quite familiar with aircraft. Both he and Reina are totally convinced that they saw something very unusual. They are reluctant to call it a spaceship, but their very clear observations left little room for misperception. They know what they saw, and it was definitely not a conventional aircraft. Again, the witnesses struggle valiantly to describe the very unusual appearance of the object.

After the sighting, Reina and Bruce drove home and told their story to their family. They told other people in Topanga and elsewhere about their sighting. Most people believed them and a few even offered stories of their own sightings.

One month later, in mid-August, 1994 at around 9:30 P.M., two San Fernando Valley residents were driving through Topanga Canyon when they saw a large white globe of light hovering over Henry Ridge on the northern edge of Topanga Canyon. The witnesses were Phillip and Mandy, who had both seen UFOs in Topanga Canyon on two previous occasions in 1992. They often drove through the canyon at night, on the way back from dinner parties with friends. Because of this, they kept putting themselves in the right place at the right time to see a UFO. Still, they weren't quite prepared for a third encounter.

They headed north on Topanga Canyon Boulevard when they saw the light. Phillip recalled, "I looked over to the left and there was a bright light that looked almost like a landing beacon of an airplane hovering in the sky. We pulled over and popped the top off the car. I got out and took a look. And it just sort of hung there. But the thing that was peculiar was, we got back in the car and continued our descent into the valley, and it seemed as if it was following us parallel. I know this can be a visual phenomenon, but it continued long enough for me to say that it wasn't a light sitting on a pole or something like that . . . it was definitely not a planet. I know what Venus looks like. I know what Jupiter looks like, and it wasn't an airplane because it was relatively stable in the sky for quite some time . . . but it was interesting and unusual enough that we did stop and look."

Mandy is also convinced that the light they saw was not easily explained. "What was really odd about this thing was that it was extremely bright, just extremely bright, and relatively low in the sky as compared to the stars, and completely motionless and silent . . . it was very clear to me that it wasn't a star and it wasn't a planet. It was just too big."

Mandy was even more impressed because the evening before, she had seen the exact same thing from her backyard in the San Fernando Valley. This fact would seem to indicate that the case may have been a close encounter with, if not Venus, perhaps a very bright star. However, both witnesses are adamant in their belief that it was not a star or planet. Venus had already set by that hour. Their story is also supported by the following case.

Therapist Linda Jordan has a friend who owns a house up Old Topanga Canyon and they often spend evenings together there. She has always been interested in UFOs, but had never seen one. She was about to see her first UFO.

One evening in mid-August, Linda and her friend were in the bedroom when their attention was drawn to a huge bright globe of white light hovering outside. It was 11:30 P.M. Linda recalled, "There's a lot of windows in my friend's house, and through one of the side windows in his bedroom, all of a sudden, there was this huge bright light. And I said to him, 'Look at that!' And he sat up and said, 'Wow! What's that?' And I got up out of bed. And he said, 'You're going to go outside, aren't you?' And I said, 'Yes!'"

The two witnesses stared at the light through the trees, but neither of them were able to identify it. As Linda remembered, "We watched it for a few minutes, and it was not moving. And it was much, much too bright to be a star. I was just about positive about that fact . . . it was bright enough to make us both get up and go outside to look, and we've never done that before. It was not a plane, because there are always a lot of planes that we see from his deck, and a lot of planes I've seen from his deck coming towards me. So I ruled that out after a few minutes. You see, the thing is, he's very skeptical, and he thought it was unusual. It wasn't just me saying, 'Wow! Look at that!' [He was] feeling the same way."

After several minutes of watching the light, they returned inside. When they looked back about fifteen minutes later, right before going to bed, the light was gone.

These reports proved to me that the Topanga Canyon UFO wave was still going strong. I summarized the reports in a brief article for the *Messenger*. Colin Penno agreed to publish the article and it appeared in the May 17, 1995 edition. Just as I suspected, the article prompted more new witnesses to step forth and tell of their own encounters. With the new encounters, the story began to take an even more bizarre turn.

17

Anomalous Lights and Strange Creatures

$\mathcal{E}$VERY TIME I thought the encounters were waning, in came a new flood of calls. Two new calls came as a result of the article about the 1994 sightings. One report was a somewhat typical case involving three witnesses who saw a mysterious star-like object. The second case, however, was much more unusual and involved a woman who, on two separate occasions, saw an unidentified creature moving across the road. I had heard of sightings of other strange creatures in UFO hotspots, but this was the first report I had coming from Topanga Canyon. I hardly knew what to expect next.

The first report came from long-time Topanga resident Eric Andrews. Andrews owns and operates a concrete laying business, and is from a large family that is well-known in the canyon. It was one evening in 1976, when he and two of his friends saw something they will never forget.

As Andrews recalled it, "We were four-wheel driving up on Henry Ridge . . . It was muddy toward Old

Canyon, so we got stuck. We were walking back about three in the morning and we saw a big, bright, bright light up in the sky . . . It was moving real slow. It was just kind of hovering. It was so high up there, but it was a bright, bright light, bigger than a star, bigger than a plane. It was just a bright, bright light and I don't know any other way to describe it. It looked like a bright star but then it was moving around. And it was too low to be a star . . . it was kind of hovering around. We were just checking it out. It seemed like it was there for about a minute or so, and it wasn't too bright to be a—it wasn't a plane. And it wasn't anything I've ever seen before.

"And right after about a minute that we were checking it out, it did like a big U-turn, but it kind of left a trail behind it. And then it took off at an incredible speed. Something like I have never ever seen and I'll never forget it. I think it was a UFO. And the guys I was with, we all still think it was a UFO . . . the way it took off, it did like a quick U-turn, a big horseshoe turn, and left a trail behind . . . and it was gone. It went off towards the valley."

Andrews and his friends were absolutely stunned by the experience. Because it was so late and they were in an isolated area, the experience was even more eerie. Andrews was the first to admit that it made him a little anxious.

"It was a chilling experience. It gave me goosebumps. It was three in the morning, and I was way out [in] the middle of nowhere. There were no houses anywhere. I totally believe in UFOs, so if somebody was to tell me I'm full of shit, that's their own thing. I've seen one. I don't have any abduction stories or cars being lifted up, but just what I think. Unless it was some kind of military test. But this was just too out of the ordinary. It was really bizarre. It gave me goose-bumps. It gave me the chills, that's for sure."

Andrews told nobody except close friends and family about the sighting. But when he kept reading about more and more sightings in the *Messenger,* he decided it was time to share his own sighting. Since then, he hasn't seen anything else unusual in the canyon, but promised to report any new sightings.

The other response from the *Messenger* article came from Mimi Smith, who has been a resident of Topanga Canyon for over forty years. Mimi is rather skeptical of the reports coming from the canyon. The only strange light she ever saw turned out to have a conventional explanation. Upon closer examination of a huge glowing bright light, Mimi realized she was seeing lights from a movie set.

Mimi is very familiar with the area. She has driven the twisting, winding roads and has seen the numerous types of wildlife that inhabit the area. Late one night in November 1994, she saw something she had never seen before: an unidentified creature. It looked to her vaguely like a sheep, but was definitely not a sheep. There were many strange details about it, but there was one particular detail that gave Mimi the shock of her life. The creature had holes for eyes!

Mimi recalled, "I'm coming home between eleven-thirty and twelve midnight, and as I pulled down the grade going into the canyon, I saw what appeared to be an animal in the street. I slammed on the brakes and pulled over to the side. It appeared to be like a sheep. Let me tell you, it was very strange. It was on the side of the road, and it was standing there. It was shaped like a sheep, and its head was round and placed lower on its body, and it appeared almost as if it had waggled on some kind of spring.

"So I waited and it crossed the road. And it didn't go with footsteps. It moved like it glided along. As I looked at it, I saw that its eyes . . . were like holes, with nothing there. You could see through. If you looked at the thing's eyes, you could see the fence posts in back of it. In other words, it was like they were hollow. There weren't any eyes. It had round holes. And it had a little mouth, you know how some dogs have brownish lips. And then [the creature] just kept right on going. It went down the other side of the mountain. And it was one of the strangest thing I have ever seen up here. We've been up here for thirty-seven years, and we've ridden the mountains a lot and seen a lot of things."

Mimi is certain that she saw something very unusual. She has seen bobcats, fox, coyote, raccoons, and all the other kinds of wildlife. She insisted this was none of those. Not only did it have holes in its head where its eyes should be, but there were other strange details. "When I put on the brakes, I thought somebody's sheep had gotten out, that was my very first thought. It was dirty-white, all funky-dirty, made out of like dirty cotton. It looked like a real dirty sheep. The hair was—it wasn't hair like we're thinking of hair. Think of a thing made of a closely densely packed fog. And then the eyes, it looked right at me, walked across and just looked right at me. My first thought, as I say, I thought it was a live animal. I slammed on the brakes.

And then I saw that it wasn't and I wasn't able to do anything. I was just transfixed with looking at it. And as it crossed to go down on the other side, I looked at its eyes, and you could see the fence posts behind its eyes, like you're looking through. I wasn't afraid. I wasn't terrified. I didn't feel like I was going to be attacked. I felt, if anything, this thing is going to take its time and I wish I wasn't here. I mean, a feeling like I don't want to mess with it. I mean, this is something, we're not talking [a] dog or sheep in the road."

After the creature crossed the road, Mimi quickly accelerated the car and raced home. She immediately told her husband who believed her but, like she, had no idea what it could be. She later consulted a Chumash Elder who suggested that it might have been a spirit woken up by all the new construction activity in the Santa Maria area of Topanga.

Mimi had no idea what she saw, but she speculated that it might be a spirit. "I realized with a shock that you could see the places where its eyes were. I realized you could look right through its eyes. I don't know. I just think it was some kind of very bizarre spirit. I know they abound in the canyon. I know other people have seen lots of other strange things like that."

I have interviewed several people in Topanga who insist that they live in haunted houses, including several people whose homes were built over and adjacent to a Chumash Indian burial ground. I have only included Mimi's account because of reports of strange creatures in other UFO hotspots. Whether or not the case is related to UFOs is pure speculation. Certainly it is part of the mystique of Topanga Canyon.

A few months after her encounter with the creature, Mimi was driving late at night through the same area when she saw the same creature again. The sighting was more brief, but again, the creature looked at her and she was amazed to see that it had holes for eyes. She knows it sounds ridiculous, but she insists she was not misperceiving and is only reporting what she saw.

Mimi is certainly not alone. Although to date, nobody else has reported seeing the same creature, many other people have seen many other strange things. As the investigation continued, every now and then I would get small clues that I had only touched the tip of the iceberg when it came to the actual number of encounters in Topanga. It was only after I put all these clues together that the whole picture became totally clear. What the picture revealed even I found hard to believe.

18

Anatomy of
a Cover-up

Is Topanga Canyon *really* a UFO flap area?

Topanga has fulfilled all ten of the qualifications of a UFO flap area. The number of encounters is astronomical. Topanga Canyon has all the elements of a UFO flap area.

While investigating the encounters, I began receiving small clues, hints, and intimations that there were many more encounters occurring over Topanga Canyon than I had previously thought. I had already investigated nearly a hundred separate encounters. But then further events seemed to indicate that there were a lot more than a few hundred encounters. These hints came in a huge variety of forms including television news stories, television talk shows, magazine articles, books, and most of all, from the Topanga Canyon UFO eyewitnesses themselves. These were not only stories of other sightings and encounters, but of a monumental cover-up of what was really happening.

By the time the investigation was drawing to a close, the sheer number of clues was overwhelming. These clues alone, without the investigated encounters, provided evidence that is compelling enough to convince even the thickest-skinned skeptic that something is being seen over Topanga. It soon became apparent that despite all my intensive investigative efforts, I had only touched the tip of the iceberg. Topanga was turning out to be a much bigger story than I could have ever imagined.

One of the first clues came from an old paperback book called *Flying Saucers on the Attack* by Harold T. Wilkins. In the book, I found this amazing quote: "Freda owns a house in Topanga Canyon. One night, she was waked by the flapping of the blind. She got up, looked out, and saw a silver bar hanging in the sky, quite near, with a pendulum movement, a slight movement. It hopped around here and there. It would vanish, then return, as if quartering the neighborhood, looking for something . . . a number of people have seen a round object showing different lights and colors, moving fast through the clouds, by day or night."[3]

Although no date is given, the book was published in 1954, so the encounter occurred now forty-five years ago.

Another report from the same book is attributed to Santa Monica resident Frederick G. Hehr. Hehr, an engineer, made the following observation: "On a June day in 1953 I had a unique experience. Twice in one day I saw saucers and witnessed a whole squadron of them go through various maneuvers, lasting ten minutes."[4]

Books and magazines have provided many clues as to what is happening over the Santa Monica Mountains. In Frank Scully's book *Behind the Flying Saucers,* I found another Santa Monica sighting. On Independence Day, back in 1947, two pilots, Dan J. Whelan and Duncan Underhill, were flying at 7,000 feet when they spotted an object about 2,000 feet above their plane. It appeared to be a "disk-shaped object, not spinning, but resembling a rifle practice target, forty to fifty feet in diameter, and traveling at around 400 to 500 miles an hour."[5]

An even earlier report comes from Timothy Good's book *Above Top Secret.* In 1942, a large disk-shaped object was sighted by literally thousands of Los Angeles residents. The object was the target of a massive artillery attack by the 37th Coast Artillery Brigade. Three people were killed, three died of heart-attacks, and many homes and buildings were destroyed as "the object eventually proceeded at a leisurely pace over the coastal cities between Santa Monica and Long Beach." Terrenz Sword's book, *The Battle of Los Angeles, 1942* presents an exciting moment-by-moment account of this historic encounter.[6]

There are also Malibu sightings quoted in the UFO literature. One comes from the late D. Scott Rogo's book *The Haunted Universe.* On January 21, 1976, "Gary W. Humecke was driving through the Malibu Hills just outside of Los Angeles . . . as he drove through the area, he was startled to see hovering over a gully below a huge object which he described as larger than any plane." The object was further described as being oval-shaped and having four lights on the top, four lights on the bottom and a row of flashing red lights along the center. Gary Humecke stopped his truck and got out to observe the object. At that point, the object began to execute strange maneuvers. The report continued, "After hovering for several seconds, the vehicle slowly rose at a 45 degree angle. It emitted no sound. After flying across a road which runs through the gully, it hovered again before slowly gliding over the hills bordering the gully and disappeared from view . . . the odd hovering and soundless gliding motion of the object would seem to rule out conventional aircraft."[7]

Another Malibu report comes from Robert M. Stanley, editor of *Unicus* magazine. Stanley has spent many hours hiking through Malibu and even conducts tours of what many people believe are the remains of an ancient civilization in the Santa Monica Mountains. Stanley says that on many occasions, he has seen objects in the area. "I have had over a dozen UFO sightings there with at least eight different eyewitnesses."

Stanley knows from personal experience that the Santa Monica Mountains are a UFO hotspot. "Well, even in the 'sixties, families were going down to the beach and waiting for a UFO to pass by. Many times I have wondered about the possibility of a facility being located underwater where the valley of Mu now rests. There have been many sightings by military and civilian sources of UFOs entering and leaving the ocean in that area. It's possible that they also have something going on deep inside the mountains."

Stanley has even seen physical evidence of the UFOs in the form of landing traces. "During the 1960s, people were frequently seeing UFOs flying around Malibu

. . . by the early 1970s, whole families were going down to the beach at Point Dume at night to watch the multi-colored UFOs [that] would sink under the water at times. In 1973, a swirling patterned crop circle appeared overnight in a field of wheat overlooking Zuma Beach . . . one particular family that lived in our neighborhood swore that a UFO had landed in their yard as they watched in amazement . . . then there was the man who lived on Point Dume, who woke up late one night to go to the bathroom, and witnessed a UFO flying sideways between [his house] and his neighbor's house."[8]

Well-known UFO researcher Ann Druffel (with D. Scott Rogo), author of *The Tujunga Canyon Contacts,* has investigated several cases of UFOs off the coast of Santa Monica, Topanga Canyon, and Malibu. As she writes, "The area has for at least thirty years been the scene of UFO reports of all kinds—surface sightings of hazy craft which cruise leisurely in full view of military installations, aerial spheres bobbing in oscillating flight, gigantic cloud—cigars and at least one report of an underwater UFO with uniformed occupants."[9]

On May 31, 1992, Marc Juliano of southern California was hiking in the Santa Monica mountains when he took a photograph of several objects. At the time the picture was taken, Marc saw nothing unusual. However, after the photograph was developed, he was surprised to see at least five strange objects hovering over the mountain ridge. The photo was published in *Unicus* magazine.[10]

Other people have also taken photos of UFOs over Topanga. When I first began reading about UFOs, I distinctly remember coming across an account of two military men who were conducting land surveys along Mulholland, on the north edge of Topanga Canyon. The survey involved complex measurements that required film being shot. While the measurements were being taken, a metallic disk appeared. The two men quickly set up their film camera and took thousands of feet of film of the metallic disk. After the event, they turned the film over to their superiors and never saw it again.

I have searched to find this source, but have not yet been able to locate it. I remember it clearly, however, because Topanga Canyon was specifically mentioned.

Probably the best photographs of UFOs over the Santa Monica Mountains was taken in May of 1993 by photographer and Malibu resident, Judy. Because she is a professional photographer, she always has her camera loaded and ready for any good photo opportunities. Then one night the opportunity came. It was around 9:00 p.m. when Judy's husband turned to her and said, "Look at all those helicopters."

Judy looked outside and was stunned to see nearly a dozen oval lights moving quickly across the sky. She recalled, "I opened the sliding glass door, rested my camera on my knee and took four photographs." The photographs clearly show nearly a dozen oval-shaped glowing white objects hovering over the mountains.

Judy had seen these strange lights before and didn't think much of them. This was the first time, however, she was able to photograph them. Only much later did she realize that the objects might be UFOs. "At the time, these weird lights were not a big deal. I just took the picture because I had been seeing these lights, off and on, for a long time, but this was the most I had ever seen in one grouping and I thought it was pretty phenomenal.

"As I was watching them, some would get brighter. They would change from a very pretty cream color light to a very intense red. There wasn't just light on one side versus the other side, they were like a ball of light that varied. Some of them would become fainter and even disappear and then suddenly blink back into sight. A couple of them piggy-backed each other. I remember that after I finished taking the photographs, they all blinked out at once. I just sat there and said, 'Wow! That was so neat.' And then I just forgot about the photos."

Judy had not been extremely excited by the lights simply because she had seen them so many times before. In fact, in July 1992, one month after the Topanga Canyon wave had begun, Judy and her friend had a remarkable sighting of what appeared to be the same objects. Judy remembered, "We were standing in the front yard, enjoying the view, and she said, 'Oh, wow, look at that!' There were five of the exact same lights that I later photographed in May of 1993. They were even the same color."

As the two witnesses watched, the objects flew back and forth at very high speeds over the mountain range, swerving towards the San Fernando valley and then swinging way back out over the ocean in literally seconds. Judy's friend cried out, "Wow, what do you think those are? I've never seen anything like that."

Judy said she didn't know, but that they should both get their binoculars. They both quickly grabbed their own binoculars and sat down to carefully observe the lights. Still, they were unable to identify them. Judy said, "They piggy-backed each other. They would get brilliant red and fade to a soft orange glow, or fade and blink on and off. I wish I knew Morse code and could correlate it to something, but it was beautiful. They ended the show by flying west toward Santa Barbara Island, which is about 50 miles from Point Dume. As they went out over the water, they were blinking on and off at once. During that time, I saw lights that would blink in, hover and then fly away. Then another would blink in, at that same area, hover for a moment and then fly off. I have come to believe that there is a safe entry way out there, a portal to another dimension."[11]

This report sounds exactly like the report given by Katherine and Daniel of their sightings which occurred exactly one month earlier. In fact, the accounts are so similar, it is obvious that these people are all seeing the same phenomenon. And as can be seen, there is considerable photographic evidence of UFOs over Topanga Canyon.

Another clue can be found in the well-known UFO documentary, *UFOs Are Real,* produced by Brandon Chase. In the documentary, retired USAF Colonel McNamara is interviewed about his own sighting. The colonel admits with frank honesty that he saw "three luminous disks over the coast of Santa Monica." According to McNamara, the objects were arranged in a triangular pattern and after about a minute, they seemed to disappear, one after the other. The sighting deeply impressed the colonel. "I feel that UFOs are real and that there are visitors on our Earth from outer space."

One of the most amazing hints of an epidemic came to light in October, 1993, on the daytime talk show *Vickie!* Why is this particular hint so amazing? Many different people have reported UFOs over Topanga, including medical doctors, military personnel, teachers, students, writers, pilots, and more. The following report, however, comes directly from the actor and Hollywood celebrity, Chad Everett. As it turns out, Everett and two other people witnessed an amazing UFO display over the Santa Monica Mountains.

Everett recalled, "There were three of us. And we were looking out from the Beverly Hills location, over Malibu. We faced that way; we could see that way. Now, at a distance which we measured to be about a yard by our arms—how many miles that would be that far away from the beach, lots right? We tracked a light that was going bump-bump-bump (he moves his hand side-to-side to illustrate the movement) and you could track it. It was making turns like that . . . nothing I know of moves like that. We called and we were told, 'There's some helicopters on maneuvers.'"

Everett said he is positive that the object was not a helicopter. He had spent some time in the Navy and is quite familiar with many types of aircraft. He said, "We couldn't actually identify a craft. We could only see this light."

Vickie Lawrence, the host of the show, asked, "A helicopter doesn't move that fast?"

"No, of course not! Of course not! No craft that we have could track that fast at that time, and make turns like that."

At the time of his appearance and interview, Everett was promoting his role in the UFO docu-drama, *Official Denial,* which tells the story of the United States government cover-up of UFO evidence. He is also the most famous of all Topanga Canyon UFO witnesses to have publicly revealed details of his encounter.

Television has provided many clues. However the strongest hints that Topanga Canyon is a UFO hotspot come not from books, magazines or television, but from eyewitnesses.

The first such hint came from two friends who as children grew up in Topanga Canyon. When I began the investigation, my first step was to ask all my friends who lived in Topanga Canyon about their experiences and possible sightings. When I asked these two friends if they had ever seen anything strange over Topanga, they had vague memories of an incident while hiking together when they saw red lights darting around the night sky. Unfortunately, the incident occurred too long ago and neither of them remember it in any real detail.

Another early but less vague report comes from a friend who told of a dramatic UFO encounter over Topanga. As she recounted it, her teenage girlfriend was riding her horse alone through Trippett Ranch when she encountered hovering lights. She was badly frightened by the lights, which were very low in the sky. She ran off on horseback, but discovered that she was missing a significant period of time. When asked if she would permit an interview, she turned pale white and said angrily, "No way!" Apparently, two such incidents occurred to this woman and the witness has done all she can to forget what happened.

That report may be slightly different or perhaps more extensive. My friend's mother is Bonnie, who saw a UFO with her family and neighbors over Santa Monica in 1980. Bonnie said of her daughter's schoolfriend, "My daughter had somebody at her school who said she was out in Malibu, down near the beach and this . . . UFO . . . because they didn't know what it was, hovered near, and then they got the real strong impression that they should leave. They had this very, very strong impression that they were supposed to leave this location. So they got out of the water and left. And then she said that she had a little triangle on her arm afterwards."

Before long, these types of hints started pouring in. A number of them came from the Fernwood/Saddlepeak area. One day I gave Topanga UFO witness Sylvia Walters the book, *Intruders*, by Budd Hopkins. She read it with great interest. Finally, an opportunity came for her to ask her next door neighbors if they had ever seen anything unusual in the sky. They looked at her in shock and then spoke of an incident that had occurred the very night before! They were all shocked by the coincidence. Her neighbors then told that the night before they were both awakened in the early morning hours by a very loud buzzing or whirring sound. The sound grew louder and louder until it sounded as if a very large object was hovering directly over the house. The sound became so loud the neighbors were just about to jump out of bed and run outside when the sound quickly faded, exactly as if a large object were leaving very quickly. They stared at each other and said, "What was that?" Neither of them could answer the question. Then, the very next day, their neighbor asks them if they've ever seen any UFOs. They were, of course, stunned.

Another report came from a friend of Colin Penno, editor of the *Messenger*. After Penno published my first article, he said a friend of his told of an incredible encounter he had along Saddlepeak. The man and his friend were driving up Saddlepeak heading towards the ocean when they saw three short figures standing by the side of the road. They looked at the figures and were shocked to see that they were only four feet tall, had huge bald heads, large almond-shaped black eyes, and grayish-white skin. They were wearing identical uniforms and were standing next to the road, looking at the witnesses as they drove by. At this point, they were within ten feet of the figures and became extremely frightened. However, they received a clear, strong telepathic message from the strange figures who said, "Do not be afraid. We won't hurt you."

Penno had been skeptical of his friend's account and asked me what I thought. I said that many people have had very similar encounters, and that the details described by his friend have been consistently reported by other people who have never met each other. The description of the figures is typical of other reports. Furthermore, telepathy is not at all uncommon in these encounters and many people who have face-to-face encounters with extraterrestrials are often given the exact same telepathic message that was given to Penno's friend. Unfortunately, Penno is no longer in touch with his friend and so the report remains just another clue that something strange has been happening in Topanga Canyon.

Another less dramatic report comes from a woman who lives along Fernwood. She heard about my interest in UFOs over Topanga and called me. Although she did discuss some of her sightings, she declined a recorded interview. But she did reveal that she lives high up along a ridgetop with a great view, and has seen hovering lights over the State Park on many occasions. I asked if she could remember any specific times and she replied that it must have happened at least a dozen times. One incident she clearly remembers was when she and her friends were all in her hot-tub late at night, admiring the view of the dark canyon and starry sky. At one point, one of them noticed bright lights hovering low over the State Park area, near Entrada. They watched for over an hour as several lights darted at right angles and hovered in place.

I received another call from a woman who has a friend who lives on Callon Drive in Topanga Canyon. Her friend told her that he once saw strange-looking lights hovering very low near his home. Unfortunately, I have never been able to interview the witness.

Another report comes from Taylor, who saw UFOs over Topanga in 1994. He reports that shortly after he moved to Topanga Canyon, a friend who had lived in the canyon asked him, "So, have you seen any UFOs yet?" Taylor replied that he hadn't, though it was obvious that his friend had. Later on, Taylor would, of course, have several dramatic encounters.

UFO investigator and author Lucius Farrish also provided a small clue. Farrish is the editor of the *UFO Newsclipping Service* and through the service, he was able to read about the Topanga Canyon sightings in the *Messenger*. He wrote to me that he distinctly remembered a contactee case occurring in Topanga Canyon. Unfortunately, it was many years ago and he was unable to locate the source.

A firsthand report comes from a woman who lives in the San Fernando Valley and works as an allergist. She reported that in mid-1992, she was driving in Woodland Hills, directly north of Topanga Canyon. She was thinking to herself how exciting it would be to see an actual UFO when suddenly she spotted a glowing disk-like object to the south, directly over the canyon. The sighting lasted mere seconds, but it was enough to convince her that she had seen an actual UFO. She could clearly see the metallic surface and the disk shape of the object in the midday sun. She preferred to remain anonymous, but insisted that her sighting is not easily explained. In fact, it propelled her to start her own UFO investigation, and she quickly uncovered dozens of new encounters in the southern California area.

One woman in Topanga told me briefly that she was in her house one evening when she saw a perfectly round-shaped craft with little lights all around the perimeter hover briefly over her home along Topanga Canyon Boulevard before the object glided away.

Another woman, a single mother who is working to become a nurse, reports seeing a pair of unexplained lights one night in Topanga Canyon. When she learned about the huge number of reports, she told her friend who lives in the canyon. Her friend said, "Oh, yeah, everybody around here knows about the UFOs."

A surprising number of UFO reports comes from the Old Topanga Canyon area. During the 1993

Topanga Days Country Fair, I distributed flyers asking for new reports. Naturally, I received several accounts. One intriguing account came from a seven-year-old boy who said that he lived near Old Canyon. The boy said that his neighbors said they had seen a UFO swoop down over their home and send down a beam of light. According to the boy, the UFO returned on a second occasion, sending down another beam of light onto the home. Shortly after, his neighbors sold their home and moved out.

Another report comes from a woman who has friends who live along Old Topanga Canyon Road. Her friends' son saw a bright blue light hovering in perfect silence over the trees, lighting up the whole area. And her friends say they know of a couple who were in their bedroom when they were awakened by an extremely bright blue-white light which lit up the whole room in a brilliant, blinding light. It lasted only a few seconds and then faded away. There was no sound during the incident.

I received another report from somebody who is a friend of a family that lives in a small trailer high on the ridge off Old Canyon Road. One evening in May 1993, she was outside of her trailer when she saw a bright red light hovering in the sky. On either side of the red light there were two smaller red lights moving in spiraling patterns. The smaller lights had the brightness of a small star, but the larger one was at least ten times larger.

Old Topanga Canyon contains a gold mine of UFO reports. Still another came from Topanga UFO witness Roger Martin, who says that his friend also saw a

UFO over Topanga. The friend declined to be interviewed, but did tell Roger many details of the sighting. As Roger reported, "They've never seen them land or get out and stuff like that. But they said they have seen things flying over. Barbecuing at night, my friend saw it one time. And he said, right on the tree-line, right above his head, it flew over, just cruising right in Old Topanga Canyon . . . he said it was disk-shaped, illuminated. You could tell the outline of it from the illumination, like lights, and metallic in the rest of the parts . . . he said it was a couple of years ago (in the early 1990s)."

Roger reported that he has two other friends who have also seen strange lights flying over Topanga Canyon. All of the witnesses, however, have declined to be interviewed due to factors involving publicity and the possible ensuing ridicule.

I have many similar reports from the Malibu area. Two separate incidents occurred in the Zuma Beach area, one involving the sighting of a metallic ship, the other involving a missing-time encounter. An in-depth study of the latter case appears in my book *One In Forty: The UFO Epidemic*. Another Topanga Canyon resident reported that his friend in Malibu had experienced several abductions out of her home.

After I distributed the flyers at Topanga Days Country Fair, one man replied that he had seen star-like lights darting across the sky several years ago while driving through Las Flores Canyon.

Four other cases came from fellow MUFON field investigator, pilot and medical doctor, Dr. David Gordon, who uncovered over one thousand brand new reports from the Los Angeles area. Dr. Gordon is the investigator who referred the case of Dr. Gordon Phillips, who saw a metallic disk accompanied by several helicopters over Topanga Canyon. Dr. David Gordon graciously volunteered to share the other cases that have occurred over the Santa Monica area. Almost all of them have occurred over Malibu.

One case involves a 1972 sighting by a woman of a star-like object that performed zig-zagging maneuvers and then suddenly disappeared; a sighting in 1974 by two men of a "four-foot diameter disk, amber colored," which hovered about one hundred feet away from them; a sighting in 1975 by a Malibu resident who saw a star-like object zig-zagging and hovering; and a sighting in 1981 at Leo Carrillo Beach by several teenagers who saw two red lights moving in zig-zagging patterns.

One of the most disturbing reports that I have not been able to investigate comes from the friend of a Topanga UFO witness. She is a Topanga Canyon resident, but she absolutely refuses to be interviewed, and when you hear her story, you'll understand why. Evidently the woman experienced a series of very close encounters with extraterrestrials who came into her Topanga Canyon home. Her encounters were very numerous, and somehow there must have been other witnesses because as a direct result of the encounters, she came under intense government surveillance. According to her friend, "There are people in our government who are still bothering her about it. That's why I was very hesitant to talk to you . . . I'm keeping her out of it completely because she's just really [upset].

She's had her phone tapped. She's being watched twenty-four hours a day. All kinds of things are going on because of it . . . she had to testify in court about it. Then people started interviewing her from I-don't-know-what-division of our government, and she's just really wigged out about it. It's just starting to calm down and she wants to keep it that way."

Unfortunately I was unable to obtain any more information on this disturbing case, but I have no reason to doubt its veracity. The report shocked me and caused me to suspect some division of our government is perfectly aware of what is going on in Topanga Canyon. It also explained the sightings of unmarked helicopters searching the canyon on the nights when the objects have been seen.

I also recalled an incident while I was conducting a telephone interview with one of the Topanga UFO witnesses. During the interview, the telephone suddenly started making a series of strange clicking sounds and then the line became filled with considerable static. The witness said, "What's that?" I said, "I don't know." He asked if we should hang up, but I asked him to stay on the line and continue relating his account. I didn't know if the line was tapped; I just wanted to continue the interview. This sort of thing has happened several times during telephone interviews. This may all be coincidence, however, as the results of my investigation were open to anybody; all they had to do was ask. I have received literally dozens of calls from Topanga residents who had not experienced sightings, but were interested in the activity.

There were still other mysteries. One UFO witness directed me to a certain area in the State Park where there were circles of crushed grass. There were three or four patches of crushed grass, all about ten feet in diameter. The circles were not precise, nor was the grass crushed in any particular pattern. There were trails leading to some of the circles; however, at least one didn't have any trails to it, but it was only four feet in diameter. None of the patches was a perfect circle. They were all slightly different shapes. I showed them to several other people, and nobody was particularly impressed. The grass wasn't swirled or broken, just pressed down. One person thought it was done by human hands, another suggested animals. The circles are strange, but it is hard to say what actually caused them. I can say that I haven't seen patches like them before or since.

All the above reports definitely strengthen the case that Topanga is a UFO hotspot. However, I also received alarming indications that the majority of UFO reports from Topanga Canyon were actually being covered-up! Confirmation of this came from an unusual source. I spoke with the Malibu Police on three occasions. They verified that they had received several calls on June 14, 1992, and that they receive UFO reports regularly throughout the year. However, they told me that the sightings are infrequent, occurring only a few times a year.

According to the police tape of the incident that occurred on June 14, 1992, when each witness called to report a UFO, they asked if there were any other calls concerning UFOs. On each occasion, the officer on duty replied in the negative.

It was only through a remarkable coincidence that the unusual events of June 14, 1992 were revealed at all.

The tape was actually leaked by an anonymous inside source. Otherwise, the entire Topanga Canyon UFO wave may have gone unnoticed by mainstream media.

Are the police perpetrating a cover-up? On June 15, 1992, Topanga Canyon UFO witnesses, Daniel and Katherine called up the police to report their sighting and ask if there were any other calls. The witnesses were genuinely upset by what they saw and turned to the police for help. The police denied having any information whatsoever, but then turned around and asked them for a detailed description of what they saw as well as for drawings!

However, when I called the police, they did confirm the June 14, 1992 incident. Another Malibu UFO witness who called the police to report his sighting was also told that there had been a series of sightings on June 14. The police graciously referred three people to me who first called them to report their sightings. In this regard, they have been very helpful. And in defense of the police, the UFO reports must represent a publicity nightmare. For example, the television program *Unsolved Mysteries* had heard about the sightings and considered producing a segment, however, they wanted an interview with a police officer. When one officer asked his superior if he could appear in uniform on television to talk about the sightings, his superior ruled against it.

When I talked to the police, they said that the UFO sightings were rare, occurring only a few times a year. Then I heard a different story.

Topanga is a small town and, as everyone knows, news travels fast in a small town. Secrets are simply very hard to keep. One of the Topanga Canyon UFO witnesses is a friend of someone who has strong connections with the Malibu/Lost Hills Police. This friend was given an actual list by the police of all the people in Topanga Canyon who have called up and reported UFOs. As the UFO witness said, "They said there [were] over three-hundred people on the list who have had the police come out and have reports, the sheriff come out . . . I think it's just within this last year."

I was stunned by this report and asked if it was correct. Three-hundred reports in the last year? That seemed a little hard to believe. The witness replied that although he didn't see the actual list, he felt that his friend is a reputable and honest person.

The witness was telling the truth about what he heard because he was able to provide very detailed information about the June 14th incident that was not published in the *Messenger* article, due to privacy considerations. The information concerns details about the identity of the witnesses that he had no way of knowing unless his friend had access to the police tape, or a source inside the police department.

Could this be true? Are there hundreds of encounters per year? Could the police be sitting on hundreds of reports that never see the light of day? Do any of these witnesses know that there are other people seeing the same thing?

I received independent corroboration from another source. It was over a year later when I was visiting the home of another Topanga witness. Her boyfriend related to me that he was invited to a dinner party where a lady claimed to have an inside source to the

Malibu/Lost Hills Police Department. As he continued, I realized with delight that he must have been at the same dinner party that the other witness had attended! He told the same story as the other witness, almost word for word. He stated that the woman said the police had received hundreds upon hundreds of calls from residents who had seen unidentified flying objects. Again, I asked if I had heard correctly, and the man replied that "yes," the woman had said that the police receive hundreds of calls each year.

This clinched the fact that there is a cover-up of the UFOs over Topanga Canyon. For whatever reason, there must be thousands of reports sitting in a file somewhere. Why the police would do this is anybody's guess. It could be that they simply refuse to handle the UFO reports that are promptly put in the "circular file," never to be seen again. They told me and other witnesses that they do not investigate UFO sightings, period. It could be that they are unofficially collecting the reports, but because of legal considerations, the reports cannot be shared. Or it could be that they are trying to actually suppress the knowledge that Topanga is a UFO hotbed simply to protect the reputation of the community they serve and protect. Or perhaps the police are overwhelmed by the reports and helpless to do anything about it. They would certainly not want to advertise the fact that they were helpless to protect their citizens from alien abduction.

Of course there could be an endless number of reasons why these reports are not being revealed. But for whatever reason, UFO witnesses who call the police are not being told the whole truth. Most of the witnesses who call the police do so not only to provide information about UFO activity, but to find out if there are more reports. Almost without exception, the witnesses who have called the police have not been told about the high levels of UFO activity. They have not been told that there are literally hundreds of reports from reliable witnesses. They are not being told the truth. Therefore, by definition, a cover-up is taking place.

Most UFO investigators agree that very few people ever report their sightings or encounters to any official agency. Probably one or two percent of UFO witnesses are inspired to call the police, the Air Force, a UFO group or other organization. Therefore, the number of actual UFO encounters is probably one hundred times greater than what is being reported. The number of reported encounters in Topanga is over eighty, which would mean that they number anywhere from five thousand to ten thousand reports.

The most amazing fact to emerge is that some unknown agency of our government is aware of the Topanga Canyon UFO wave. They have apparently hovered over the area—searching for and chasing after—UFOs. They have tapped people's phones and may have forced at least one person to actually testify in court about her encounters! Our government, or some faction thereof, not only knows about the encounters, but has kept completely silent about them.

The evidence is undeniable. The above reports alone represent the entire range of UFO encounters. And all have occurred within the Santa Monica Mountains. And because Topanga Canyon is sandwiched between Santa Monica and Malibu and is located in the heart of the Santa Monica Mountains, it is the focus of most of the UFO activity.

The next logical question is *why* Topanga Canyon?

19

Why Topanga Canyon?

THE SINGLE MOST **common** question people ask about the Topanga Canyon UFO encounters is, "Why Topanga Canyon?" In other words, what is so special about Topanga that it should attract so many UFOs and unusual phenomena?

This, of course, is the question on my mind ever since I began the investigation. What makes Topanga different from other areas that don't have so many encounters?

Some people have asked me if it could have something to do with the residents of Topanga Canyon themselves. Yet the witnesses represent a typical cross-section of society, including pilots, teachers, students, writers, military men, a pool cleaner, a therapist, students, homemakers, the manager of a tow-truck company, a landscaper, a photographer, a magazine editor—and even a vagrant.

The only pattern related to the witnesses is that there is no real pattern. People of all types, young and old, are seeing the objects. The only real factor they

247

have in common is that they all live in Topanga Canyon.

This leads us back to the question: why Topanga Canyon? Could it be something about the geology or geography of the area? The Santa Monica Mountains have some unique aspects. Geologically, the soil is sandy and clay-like. One Topanga witness remarked upon the super-abundance of quartz in the State Park area. There are also huge outcroppings of bedrock and sandstone riddled with caves, many of which are quite large. Also, the entire range was once underwater, and a certain location up Old Topanga Canyon Road is extremely rich in fossils. After a heavy rain, literally hundreds of fossils can be found lying on the ground. Geologically, although interesting, there is really nothing outstandingly different from other areas.

Topanga Canyon's geographic location is also very interesting. Firstly, Topanga Canyon contains Topanga State Park which is the second largest inner-city State Park in the entire world, surpassed only by nearby Griffith Park. Unlike Griffith Park, which is easily accessible, Topanga is geographically isolated from the surrounding terrain. It is a very large wilderness area surrounded by the huge sprawling megalopolis of Los Angeles. The Santa Monica Mountains rise so steeply above the valley floors that building in the area was initially impossible. It was this fact alone that saved the area from becoming as populated as the rest of Los Angeles. By the time building technology had evolved to the point of being able to conquer the steep canyons, Topanga Canyon had already enacted strict building codes requiring houses to be built on parcels of land at least two acres in size. Many developers have tried to build dense suburbs in the canyon, only to be defeated by the Topanga Association for a Scenic Community. In fact, a recent development that was defeated ended up having the largest environmental impact report in the history of Los Angeles. The area, Summit Valley, which is located in north Topanga, directly south of the Top o' Topanga lookout, was subsequently purchased and added to Topanga State Park, making the park even larger than it was before.

There are literally thousands of small mini-canyons winding throughout the Santa Monica Mountains. They are unpopulated and quite remote. Many of them have such rough terrain that they are virtually inaccessible by foot. The chaparral and sagebrush grow thickly, it is nearly impossible to travel cross-country without a trail. Poison oak is also very abundant. Many factors combine to make these canyons difficult to reach. If extraterrestrials needed a place to hide while still having a large human population to work with, Topanga Canyon would be the ideal location. They could hide in Topanga undetected, then whisk off to perform their surveys, abductions, or whatever their particular tasks might be. In other words, Topanga Canyon is the equivalent of a hiding place—a blind—used by hunters or nature photographers to get as close as possible to wild animals without being detected.

In this way, Topanga Canyon is similar to the Hudson Valley, New York area. Both are very rural areas that are directly adjacent to urban centers. Still, many places have these qualifications. There may be other important factors.

Gulf Breeze, Florida, is a very well-known UFO hotspot. Many people have speculated that Gulf Breeze experiences so many UFO sightings because it is surrounded on three sides by military bases. Why UFOs would be attracted to military bases is also speculative, but investigators generally agree that the objects seem to keep tabs on how advanced our technology is. UFOs are known for hovering over highly technical installations. One well-known incident occurred in Hudson Valley, New York, where a large metallic unidentified flying object was seen by state employees hovering directly over the Indianhead Nuclear Power Plant.

The Santa Monica Mountains are not unspoiled by military installations. One is the Point Mugu Naval Station located at the far southwestern tip of the Santa Monica Mountains, along the coast. Another is the Hughes Research Center located near Pepperdine University in Malibu. Hughes Research Center is not exactly military, but it does conduct all kinds of top secret scientific research for various agencies of the United States federal government.

Coral Canyon, located in Malibu, was the location for cutting-edge research with magnetics. The area was chosen because it was free from contamination of natural magnetic influences. Today the building where the tests were conducted is preserved as a museum for tourists.

While he was governor of California, Ronald Reagan proposed using the Santa Monica Mountains as a dumping ground for toxic nuclear waste. Presumably, the mountains were close enough and yet also isolated enough for such a project. Fortunately, the idea never went beyond the first proposal and was promptly forgotten.

There are other minor installations. There are several large water tanks which hold hundreds of thousands of gallons of water to be used in brush fires. There is a large radio tower on a ridgetop along the western edge of Topanga Canyon.

Santa Monica does have an airport, but it is not located in the mountain range. Topanga Canyon itself is nowhere near military installations of any kind. There are a number of highly advanced installations in the nearby San Fernando Valley, including Rocketdyne, Hughes Aircraft and Van Nuys Air Force Reserve Base.

Some researchers have noticed connections between UFO activity and sacred sites, such as ancient ruins. Topanga Canyon just happens to be a well-known Chumash Indian settlement. It was considered a sacred area by the former residents and was used as an important meeting place for various tribes.

Evidence of the former Native American population can be found throughout Topanga Canyon. The best-known location is the Trippett Ranch area in Topanga State Park. Many residents of the area have found artifacts of all kinds. A friend of mine who lived up Entrada and I found a perfectly formed, shiny white, flint arrowhead. He donated it to a gentleman in the area who was collecting the artifacts.

There is also an actual Indian burial ground located partly in the Trippett Ranch area, and partly where some houses have been built. Several people have homes built either on or directly adjacent to the Indian burial ground. At least four of the homes in the area have reported paranormal activity, including phantom footsteps, levitating objects, and mysterious knocking sounds.

Other areas throughout Topanga are known for containing large Native American past settlements. The area behind Topanga Canyon Post Office is known to have been a settlement. Also, the caves between Santa Maria and Cheney Drive still contain stone holes used by the Chumash to grind wheat into flour.

The Santa Monica mountains may be the location of an ancient civilization. Most people are familiar with the legend of Atlantis, speculated to be off the coast of Florida, or in the Bahamas. What many people don't known is that there are similar legends of ancient civilizations on the west coast of the United States.

Robert Stanley, editor of *Unicus* magazine, has discovered what he believes are the ruins of an ancient civilization called Mu. He leads tours to certain areas in Malibu where unusual rock formations can be found.

Another gentleman used to lead tours to similar locations, but he believes that the civilization was Lemuria. Both Mu and Lemuria have been referenced in historical manuscripts. Whether Mu or Lemuria, the Santa Monica mountains may be archaeologically significant.[11]

Finally, a vortex is another possible reason that Topanga is a UFO hotspot. A vortex is an area with a high level of geo-electromagnetic energy. The most famous vortex in the United States is in Sedona, Arizona. According to Anthony, a contactee who has had two UFO sightings over Topanga Canyon, there exists an even larger vortex over Topanga Canyon. He says that he can actually see the energy from the vortex. According to him, it is a negative vortex, meaning, it rotates counter-clockwise. Also, the vortex is giant, spanning the entire Santa Monica Mountain Range including all of Topanga Canyon and Malibu, and parts of Santa Monica and Woodland Hills.

According to Anthony, the UFOs are able to use energy from the vortex as an energy source and transportation route. The vortex can also cause the objects to become visible.

To the best of my knowledge, the vortex has not been detected or measured by scientific instruments. This, of course, does not mean that the vortex does not exist. Although there may be no proof, I have no reason to doubt its existence. However, until there is further corroborative evidence, the vortex theory must remain just that—a theory.

The above speculations are the most popular theories about why Topanga Canyon is a UFO flap area. Ultimately, however, the cause remains a mystery. It could be the isolation and geography. It could have something to do with the highly technical or military installations located on the western end of the Santa Monica Mountains. It could be the indisputable archeological significance of the area. It could be the vortex. Or it could be something else entirely.

Most likely, the high levels of UFO activity is a combination of the above theories. And until more is known about UFOs and their agenda on Earth, conclusive answers to these types of questions will remain as elusive as the UFOs themselves.

Epilogue

A UFO FLAP area is a geo-graphically defined location that produces a dispro-portionately large number of UFO reports. UFO waves occur within UFO flap areas. For the ten qualifications of a UFO flap area listed earlier, Topanga Canyon ful-fills every single one.

It should be clear by now that flap areas are proba-bly not a social phenomenon. The huge number of reported encounters is a direct reflection of the huge number of actual encounters. There is a possibility that a flap area could go unnoticed due to lack of publicity. However, it is highly unlikely that the reverse would be true; that an area could become a flap area because of increased publicity. Certainly, UFO activity occurs everywhere on the planet. However, flap areas, or areas of high concentrations of UFO activity, are very real and are easily distinguishable by the many factors that make up a flap area.

Topanga Canyon is a smaller flap area than most, however, it has factors that make it more intense. The huge number of objects seen in the sky at one time is unique. And yet, multiple independent witnesses have all reported seeing over a dozen strange craft in the sky on any single occasion.

Now that Topanga Canyon has been put on the map as a flap area, there is increased publicity. The UFO witnesses continue to go about their private lives. Some wish to simply forget about their encounters and put the past behind them. Others want to know more. A few are keenly interested and are privately studying the encounters on their own.

Some of the witnesses have moved away. Others continue living as they have for decades. And others are still new to the area and are just beginning to settle in.

Topanga and Malibu had devastating wildfires in 1993, in which over two hundred homes were lost, including many very expensive homes. The Topanga witnesses also suffered some losses. Two of the witnesses on Saddlepeak lost their homes. Most Topanga Canyon residents were forced to evacuate as the wildfire swept toward the Fernwood area, where it was finally extinguished by over four-thousand firemen—almost half the population of Topanga Canyon itself. Unfortunately two people died in the fire.

After the fire there was a series of floods and mudslides further devastating Malibu and Topanga Canyon. Then, about a year later came the Northridge quake which destroyed hundreds of thousands of homes, many in Topanga, Malibu, and Santa Monica.

The Santa Monica Mountains have been the location of many fires, floods, mudslides, and other natural disasters. Somehow, however, the community always recovers, and although there are always scars, everybody comes together to heal each other and start again.

The Topanga Canyon UFO wave was by no means a natural disaster, though I am sure some residents feel that it may be a public relations disaster. The last thing anybody wants, especially someone skeptical of UFOs, is to be known for living in a UFO hotspot. For some, the encounters have surely been the source of considerable embarrassment. For many, the UFO wave has been exciting, even rewarding. For others, the wave brought only the terror of the unknown and a series of traumatic experiences they would rather forget. For still others, UFOs have brought transformation both physical and spiritual.

The UFO activity over Topanga shows all the signs of continuing. In early 1996, I received another report from five young men who were hiking in the State Park area. Two of them saw a light hover and quickly dart away at high speeds. They called after seeing my flyer. All the witnesses have said that they were relieved to know that they weren't alone. I am currently tracking down two other cases; one involving a woman who sighted an anamolous light, and another involving a man who said he was struck by a beam of light while hiking through the hills. Both incidents, of course, occurred in Topanga. I have also learned of another case involving a mother and her son, who experienced a long, complex abduction scenario in the Santa

Monica Mountains. The case, investigated by Dr. Bruce Goldberg, involves multiple abductions over many years.[12]

That has been a common theme among the UFO witnesses. Many of them told no one about their encounters for years, and were literally covering up the truth in the hopes that people wouldn't think they were crazy. Several witnesses only agreed to be interviewed after much persuasion. Some insisted on absolute anonymity. Not one of them was looking for publicity of any kind. Many of the witnesses were deeply troubled by what they saw, and a few refused to even discuss it with me at all.

It's not always easy to see an unidentified flying object. Today, Topanga Canyon residents continue to deal with the UFO encounters as best as they can. The individual witnesses struggle to accept their experiences. The families of the witnesses continue to challenge the issues of skepticism and trust that sharing a UFO encounter raises. The community itself has been deeply affected by the encounters. Its reputation as a UFO hotspot has made it the focus of much national attention. It has been the focus of books, magazine and newspaper articles as well as television and news programs.

The fact that there is some sort of cover-up of UFO activity by the United States government is agreed upon by most UFO investigators. The information uncovered in my investigation into the Topanga Canyon UFO encounters also reveals a cover-up. The local police department sit on what appear to be thousands of valid UFO reports. At least one witness in

Topanga Canyon may have become the victim of government surveillance, phone tapping and perhaps more. The fact that unmarked helicopters have been seen in conjunction with the UFOs is also very interesting. Do our authority figures know something about UFOs over Topanga Canyon that they're not telling us? Obviously, yes. This is demonstrably true in regards to the police and evidently true when it comes to our own government.

Ultimately, however, the cover-up is our own fault. We are ultimately responsible for the behavior of our own government. If there is a cover-up, the truth is already largely known anyway. In either case, we pay the price. The Topanga UFO witnesses who have undergone extremely extensive encounters must struggle with little or no support from authorities. Many times, their only consolation is knowing that others have undergone similar experiences. Often, it's a long road to finding the right person to talk to. Many UFO witnesses have nobody to turn to, nobody to tell their story, nobody from whom to learn more information.

When the first UFO article was published in the *Messenger*, I don't think anybody had any idea how big the story would become. When the flap began a couple of years later and the reports poured in, I investigated each one in turn, and even wrote another article at the request of Colin Penno, editor of the *Messenger*. Penno stated his desire to print the article but was shocked to find out that there were so many new cases, with information totaling over sixty pages, certainly too much for a small hometown newspaper. He asked me to write an eight-page article and he would try to place it in an upcoming issue.

By now, the story was so big that the reports were coming in faster than they could be published. When the article finally came up for consideration, one of the editors of the *Messenger* (who requested to remain anonymous), felt that UFOs were tabloid material and would hurt the quality of the newspaper. Penno put up a battle, but the editor wouldn't budge. The UFO story had gotten out of control. Nobody wanted to hear about hundreds of UFOs seen by multiple witnesses. If it were a story of a single sighting, it may have passed. But it wasn't. And the story was growing more complicated by the day.

Eventually another severely edited article was printed and it did elicit some response. Penno has also stated his desire to print more articles in the future. If there is a cover-up, the *Messenger* is certainly not a part of it. Furthermore, credit again must be given to the Malibu/Lost Hills Police Department who were in the very awkward and unenviable position of being in a UFO flap area and dealing with a UFO wave. As I stated earlier, the whole wave may have gone unnoticed, if not for the one leak in the police department which revealed the tape of the reports received on June 14, 1992. Although the great majority of reports was covered up, the truth leaked out.

Now that Topanga Canyon is a known UFO hotspot, I know several residents who have video cameras ready and waiting. Startling videotape has already been taken in other UFO flap areas including Gulf Breeze, Florida, and Hudson Valley, New York. This has nearly happened in Topanga Canyon more than once, and if the encounters continue as they have been, it won't be long before somebody obtains some outstanding videotape or film footage.

The Topanga Canyon encounters do seem to have slowed down, though every time I put up new flyers, it brings in at least one report. My guess is that the encounters will continue and that soon there will be another wave of activity. That has been the pattern in other UFO hotspots.

Appendix:
Chronology and Analysis

TOPANGA CANYON REPRE-
SENTS a microcosm of UFO activity around the world.
The encounters include all types and number easily in
the hundreds. They have occurred to all kinds of people for well over forty years. The only truly unique
aspect of the encounters, other than being original
firsthand accounts, is that they have all occurred in
virtually the same location (see Figure 2, next page).

With so many encounters occurring so regularly for
so many years, certain patterns have become apparent.

What follows is a chronology of the encounters.
Each case includes the date and time, the precise location, the names and number of the witnesses and a
short description of the encounter. Only those cases
with sufficient data for analysis have been included.

**February 25, 1942. Evening. Santa Monica and Los
Angeles.** Large disk-shaped object hovered high in the
sky, witnessed by thousands of people, and was fired
upon by the U.S. military. Several people were killed

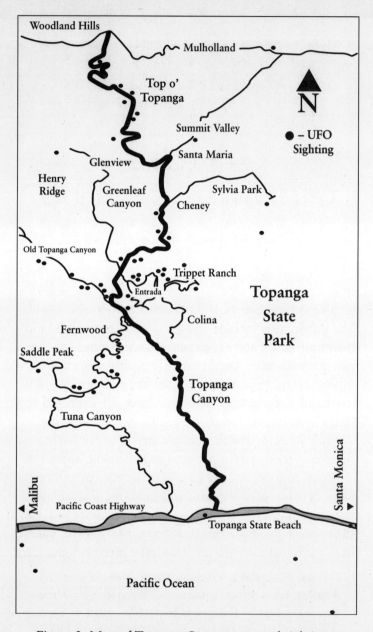

Figure 2: Map of Topanga Canyon area and sightings.

by debris and died of heart attacks. Object was observed for several hours before moving slowly away.

1947. Day. Santa Monica. Two witnesses: Dan Whelan and Duncan Underhill. Witnesses were flying at 7,000 feet when they observed a disk-shaped craft moving at about 500 miles per hour.

Early 1950s. Evening. Topanga Canyon. One witness: Freda. Witness observed a silver bar-shaped object hovering and darting back and forth. Possible other witnesses.

1953. Day. Santa Monica. One witness: Frederick G. Hehr. Witness observed a "squadron of saucers" performing maneuvers. Objects were observed on two separate occasions on the same day, lasting about ten minutes each.

Summer 1961 or 1962. Afternoon. Grandview Drive, Topanga Canyon. Three witnesses: Beverly Smith and her two daughters, Lisa and Kim. Three metallic disks observed hovering over Topanga State Park. Witnesses experience a period of missing time. Objects were observed for fifteen minutes.

1960s. Beverly Hills. Three witnesses: Actor Chad Everett and two others. Witnesses observed a bright light darting back and forth at high speeds over the ocean, Topanga Canyon, and Malibu for a duration of several minutes from the location of Beverly Hills, immediately east of Topanga Canyon.

1972. Evening. Malibu. One witness: anonymous. Witness observed a star-like darting object which disappeared after a few minutes.

Summer 1973 or 1974. Santa Maria, Topanga Canyon. Three witnesses: Johnny X and two friends. Star-like objects observed hovering and darting over the State Park. Objects observed for about one hour.

Summer 1974. 4:30 A.M. Old Topanga Canyon Road, Topanga Canyon. Two witnesses: Kim Smith and her friend. Star-like object was observed darting across the sky. Object was observed for five seconds.

Summer 1974. 10:00 P.M. Fernwood Pacific Drive at Saddlepeak, Topanga Canyon. Two witnesses: Sylvia Walters and friend. Egg-shaped lighted object observed hovering over ridgeline for about five seconds. Object emitted low buzzing sound.

1974. Evening. Piuma, Malibu. Two witnesses: anonymous. Witness observed a four-foot amber-colored disk hovering one hundred feet away.

May 1975. 5:30 A.M. Santa Monica Freeway and Pacific Coast Highway, Santa Monica. Three witnesses: George Gray (pseudonym), his sister, and her boyfriend. Silver disk-like object was observed hovering and emitting a colorful beam of light. Object was observed for fifteen minutes. Possible telepathic communication with object.

1975. Evening. Piuma, Malibu. Two witnesses: Robert P. and his wife. Orange globe of light observed floating in sky for a duration of eleven seconds.

1975. Sunset. Piuma, Malibu. One witness: Robert P. Red ball of light observed moving quickly across the sky for a duration of five seconds.

1975. Evening. Malibu. One witness: anonymous. Witness observed a star-like object zigzag and hover for a few seconds.

January 21, 1976. Evening. Malibu. One witness: Gary W. Humecke. Witness observed an oval-shaped object with colored lights hovering and gliding over a gully.

Winter 1976. 3:00 A.M. Henry Ridge, Topanga Canyon. Three witnesses: Eric Andrews and two friends. Witnesses were walking home through a secluded area when they observed a star-like object perform seemingly impossible maneuvers before quickly departing. Object was observed for five seconds.

1977. Evening. Piuma, Malibu. One witness: Robert P. Yellow-orange globe of light observed floating in sky for a duration of two seconds.

October 1978. Evening. Piuma, Malibu. One witness: Robert P. The witness was lying in bedroom when he was paralyzed by a buzzing vibration. Three days later, a circular ring appeared in his backyard and the top of witness's pine tree was snapped off. Buzzing sound was heard for two minutes. Case involves possible missing time.

1979. Evening. Piuma, Malibu. One witness: Robert P. Witness was resting in room when he sensed a presence outside. He planned to investigate but suddenly fell unconscious. The next day, another ring appeared in his backyard. Missing time.

1970s. Evening. Fernwood Pacific Drive, Topanga Canyon. Several witnesses: anonymous. A resident reports that she and her friends observed strange lights darting and hovering over Topanga State Park. The lights were observed for more than an hour.

June 1980. 8:00 P.M. Pacific Coast Highway, Malibu. Two witnesses: Linda Susan Young and friend. Bright light was observed rising off the ocean's surface. Object was observed for about five minutes.

Summer 1980. 9:00 P.M. Santa Monica. Seven witnesses: Donald and Bonnie, their three children, and two neighbors. Red glowing object in the shape of a half-circle was observed (using binoculars) hovering in the sky for a duration of ten minutes. An identical object was observed two days later by four new witnesses.

1980. 5:00 P.M. Santa Monica. Two witnesses: Toshi Inouye and his student. Red cigar-shaped object was observed from an airplane hovering over the mountain range. Object was observed for thirty seconds. An identical object was observed a few days later by the student and his friends who reported that the object chased them in their car along the mountain roads.

1981. Midnight. Piuma, Malibu. One witness: Robert P. Blinking, star-like red light observed high in sky for a duration of fifteen minutes, three days in a row.

1981. Evening. Malibu. Two witnesses: anonymous. Witnesses observe two red star-like lights move in zigzagging patterns.

1982. Evening. Piuma, Malibu. One witness: Robert P. Star-like object observed making right-angle turns. Object was observed for one minute.

1982. Evening. Piuma, Malibu. One witness: Robert P. Bright green light was observed overtaking and passing a jet. Object was observed for twelve seconds.

1982. 1:00 A.M. Mulholland Highway (east of Topanga Canyon Boulevard), Topanga Canyon. Two witnesses: Mark Grant and friend. Three lights observed hovering in a triangular formation. Lights then swooped down towards the witnesses and changed color and position. Lights were observed for fifteen minutes. Possible missing time.

April or May 1986. 11:00 P.M. Lower Encina Road, Topanga Canyon. Three witnesses: Gabe Aldort, Vadja Potenza and A. W. Two star-like objects observed rotating around each other and departing in opposite directions. Objects were observed for five seconds.

February 1987. 11:00 P.M. Old Topanga Canyon Road, Topanga Canyon. Four witnesses: Gabe Aldort, John Heldman, Ivan Eason, Leif Eason. One small solid-looking object with lights observed passing overhead, followed by two similar objects. A fourth very large object was observed casting down a beam of light and was followed by a fifth smaller object. Large object emitted buzzing sound and was transparent upon departure. Objects observed for ten minutes.

Summer 1988. Malibu. One witness: Kim Carlsberg. Witness observes a star-like object move back and forth across the ocean from her coastside home. At one point, the object darts towards the witness to a distance of only a hundred feet. Witness reports the object was at least fifty feet in diameter. Possible telepathic communication with object. Sighting lasted for one minute.

1989. 6:00 P.M. Malibu. Two witnesses: Linda Susan Young and friend. Metallic disk-shaped object was observed moving slowly and silently between the canyon ridges for a duration of thirty seconds.

Late 1980s. Evening. Old Topanga Canyon Road, Topanga Canyon. One witness: anonymous. Witness observed a disk-like craft with lights moving slowly over the treetops.

Late 1980s–Early 1990s. Evenings. Malibu. One witness: Kim Carlsberg. Witness has experienced numerous abductions out of her Malibu home. She has had encounters with several types of aliens, has experienced medical procedures, and been presented with babies. She also has been taken to a human-made underground base occupied by humans and aliens working together. Witness reports telepathic communication with entities.

1990. Evening. Saddlepeak, Topanga Canyon. Two witnesses: anonymous. Two witnesses were awakened by a buzzing sound over their home which increased in intensity and then faded away. Encounter lasted for twenty seconds.

January 1991. Pre-dawn hours. Entrada, Topanga Canyon. One witness: Susan. Bedroom visitation during which witness was unable to move, speak, or see. Witness sensed a presence which snipped off a lock of her hair, probed her body with a pencil-like instrument and then departed. Encounter lasted for a few minutes.

Early 1991. 3:30 A.M. Pacific Coast Highway, Malibu. One witness: Tony. Prism-like light was observed floating on ocean's surface for a duration of fifteen minutes.

1991. Afternoon. Topanga Canyon Boulevard, Topanga Canyon. Two witnesses: Mark and Christine Dennett. A blue star-like light was observed descending slowly over the Old Topanga Canyon area for a duration of three seconds.

May 13, 1992. 11:00 P.M. Piuma, Malibu. Two witnesses: Robert P. and his wife. Bright globe of white light was observed hovering and descending behind a ridge. Object was observed for ten seconds. Witnesses meditated the day before with the objective of seeing a UFO; possible telepathic communication with object.

May 31, 1992. Day. Malibu. Two witnesses: Marc Juliano and Robert Stanley. Juliano took photographs of hillside. Neither witness saw anything, but the photos taken clearly show what appear to be several objects hovering in the sky.

June 14, 1992. 8:30–10:30 P.M. Saddlepeak, Topanga Canyon. Two witnesses: Daniel and Katherine. Over two hundred oval-shaped glowing objects were observed rising from behind a ridge, one by one. Objects darted across the sky in different directions, sometimes darting at right angles. Objects were observed for over two hours.

June 14, 1992. After midnight. Topanga Canyon Boulevard, Topanga Canyon. Two witnesses: anonymous. A bright object followed car and levitated it off the road. Missing time. Object observed for five minutes.

June 14, 1992. After midnight. Topanga Canyon Boulevard, Topanga Canyon. Two witnesses: anonymous. Three flying disks followed witnesses as they drove through canyon. Witnesses got out of car to observe the objects which quickly departed. Objects observed for five minutes.

June 14, 1992. After midnight. Two witnesses: anonymous. Witnesses were awakened by a bright light hovering over their home, lighting up their bedroom. Object emitted buzzing noise. Object was observed for two minutes.

June 14, 1992. After midnight. Topanga Canyon Boulevard, Topanga Canyon. One witness: anonymous. A bright object followed witness as he drove south along the boulevard. Object was observed for five minutes.

June 14, 1992. After midnight. Callon Drive, Topanga Canyon. One witness: Dr. Murray Clarke. A star-like object was observed moving quickly across the sky for a duration of five seconds.

June 14, 1992. After midnight. Topanga Canyon Boulevard, Topanga Canyon. Witness observed bright beams of light flashing downward from the sky for a duration of several minutes.

June 14, 1992. 12:30 A.M. Topanga Canyon Boulevard, Topanga Canyon. Two witnesses: Phillip and Mandy. Several disk-like objects observed over Topanga Canyon for a duration of fifteen minutes.

June–July, 1992. 11:00 P.M. Topanga Canyon Boulevard, Topanga Canyon. Two witnesses: Janice and her boyfriend, John. On four separate occasions, bright flashes of light were observed while driving through the canyon. Each sighting lasted for about three seconds.

June 20–23, 1992. 1:00–3:00 A.M. Entrada, near Topanga State Park, Topanga Canyon. Roger and Sarah Martin. Three nights in a row, a metallic disk was seen hovering outside the witnesses' home. A buzzing sound was emitted by object. All animal sounds stopped while the object was present. Sarah reports a UFO "dream" involving entities. Two types of metallic craft were seen. Objects were observed for up to forty-five minutes. Telepathic communication was reported by both witnesses.

July 4, 1992. 8:00 P.M. Topanga Canyon Boulevard, Topanga Canyon. Two witnesses: Roger Martin and his brother James. A very large object with red lights was observed by witnesses hovering over Topanga Canyon for a duration of five minutes.

July 1992. 1:30 A.M. Entrada, near Topanga State Park, Topanga Canyon. One witness: Roger Martin. Witness was awakened by the familiar buzzing sound of the UFO when he observed a Volkswagon Beetle being followed up the street by a small saucer-shaped object. Object was observed for about five seconds.

July 14, 1992. 11:00 P.M. Topanga State Park, Topanga Canyon. Four witnesses: Phillip, Mandy, Anthony, Susan. Star-like object(s) were observed darting and flashing for a duration of thirty minutes.

July 14, 1992. 1:00–2:00 A.M. Charmlee Park, Malibu. Two witnesses: Anthony and friend. Six teardrop-shaped lights were observed maneuvering over the ocean for a duration of one hour.

Third week in July 1992. 1:00–3:00 A.M. Entrada, near Topanga State Park, Topanga Canyon. Two witnesses: Roger and Sarah Martin. Witnesses were awakened by a buzzing sound. All animal sounds stopped. Object returned three days in a row. Roger observed two different types of craft. Possible telepathic communication between UFO and witnesses. The first two nights, the object stayed for at least fifteen minutes. On the third night, the object left after fifteen seconds.

July 1992. 1:00–3:00 A.M. Entrada, near Topanga State Park, Topanga Canyon. Two witnesses: Roger and Sarah Martin. Witnesses were awakened by the buzzing sound of the UFOs about twice a week throughout the month. Animal sounds stopped. Buzzing noise was heard for about fifteen minutes on each occasion, although no object was observed. Military helicopters also were observed hovering over the area.

July 1992. Evening. Malibu. Two witnesses: Judy and friend. Witnesses observe (using binoculars) several oval-shaped glowing objects which move in darting patterns across the sky.

Second week in August, 1992. 1:00–3:00 A.M. Entrada, near Topanga State Park, Topanga Canyon. Two witnesses: Roger and Sarah Martin. Object returned again for three nights in a row and was observed by Roger. Animal sounds stopped. Buzzing noise was again emitted by object.

August 16, 1992. 5:30 P.M. Pacific Coast Highway, Malibu. Two witnesses: Adam and Mario. Five or six black, diamond-shaped objects observed in a circular formation hovering over the ocean and darting at high speeds for a duration of about one minute.

August 1992. 9:00 P.M. Topanga Canyon Boulevard, Topanga Canyon. One witness: Preston Dennett. Witness observed a bright star-like object hover and disappear. Light was observed for five seconds.

September 22, 1992. Midnight. Topanga Canyon Boulevard, Topanga Canyon. Two witnesses: Ethan Holtzman and an unidentified vagrant. Witness was driving north on the boulevard when he observed a large red object descending vertically into the creek. Object was observed for about five seconds. Witness reports that object landed exactly where a fatal motorcycle accident had previously occurred.

October 1992. 10:00 P.M. Los Flores Canyon Road, Malibu. One witness: Eric Beckjord. Pulsating bright light was seen hovering over ridgeline for a duration of one minute.

1992. Day. Woodland Hills. One witness: anonymous. Witness observed a glowing disk-like object hovering over Topanga Canyon for a duration of about five seconds.

January 1993. 3:30 A.M. Pacific Coast Highway, Malibu.
One witness: Tony. Prism-like light observed floating
on ocean's surface for a duration of fifteen minutes.

**March 7–8, 1993. 9:30 P.M.–1:00 A.M. Grandview
Drive, Topanga Canyon.** One witness: Valerie Dennett.
Two nights in a row, Valerie observed a star-like object.
On the second night, the star-like object winked out
and was replaced by red and blue lights. Two similar
objects were observed. Objects were observed for at
least three hours. Witness reports that the objects
changed color when she wished upon them, thinking
they were stars, and also feels that the objects were
observing her: possible telepathic communication with
objects.

**Early May 1993. 9:00 P.M. Old Canyon Road, Topanga
Canyon.** One witness: anonymous. Witness observed a
red globe of light and two smaller red star-like lights
performing spiraling maneuvers on opposite sides of the
larger red globe. Lights were observed for five minutes.

May 1993. Evening. Malibu. Two witnesses: Judy and
her husband. Witnesses observe several oval-shaped
glowing objects darting in the sky above the mountains. Judy quickly snapped four photos, two of which
clearly show nearly a dozen of the objects.

**May 26–27, 1993. 9:00 P.M.–1:30 A.M. Kanan Road,
Malibu.** Two witnesses: Chuck and Karen. A bright
star-like object was observed with several red lights
darting around it. Objects were observed for nearly five
hours. Objects were observed for two days in a row.

Summer 1993. 1:00 A.M.–3:00 A.M. Entrada, near Topanga State Park, Topanga Canyon. Two witnesses: Roger and Sarah Martin. Witnesses report that throughout the summer, they heard the familiar buzzing sound of a UFO outside their home. Animal sounds ceased on each occasion. Witnesses reported at least a dozen such encounters, each one lasting anywhere from five to twenty minutes, or longer.

September 18, 1993. 2:30 A.M. Fernwood Pacific Drive, Topanga Canyon. One witness: Dr. David Phillips. Witness observed three helicopters and two motor vehicles searching for something in Topanga State Park. He was wondering what they were looking for when he saw a large, shiny, metallic, disk-shaped craft moving quickly south above the boulevard but below the level of the mountains. The object was observed for no longer than five seconds.

October 18, 1993. 3:00 A.M. Grandview Drive, Topanga Canyon. One witness: Valerie Dennett. Witness observed a white and red light swoop down in a strange motion and then move quickly away. Lights were observed for five seconds.

November 21, 1993. 9:00 P.M. Topanga Canyon Boulevard, Topanga Canyon. Two witnesses: Michael and Helen Thompson. Witnesses observe four bright circles of light moving in spiraling patterns in the clouds above. Lights were observed for twenty minutes. Possible animal effects during that month including strange behavior from their dog and unidentifiable wounds on their horses.

January 17, 1994. Topanga Canyon Boulevard and the Top o' Topanga Trailer Park, Topanga Canyon. Two witnesses: Marcellina and Lewis. Witnesses observe over fifty small objects moving in rows across the sky. They later see a huge transparent object towing a smaller object. Later, Marcellina sees several white glowing objects. A strange buzzing noise was heard from some of the objects. A few weeks after encounter, Marcellina experienced a visitation with a gray-type entity. Telepathic communication occurred and Marcellina was given information about the aliens, about healing, and other predictions. Shortly after she became pregnant and experienced a missing fetus. She later experienced at least two miraculous healings.

February 1994. 11:00 P.M. Entrada, Topanga Canyon. One witness: Samantha. Witness observed red lights moving in strange geometric patterns. Experience may be more extensive than a sighting.

March 1994. Evening. Topanga Canyon Boulevard near the Top o' Topanga, Topanga Canyon. One witness: Taylor. Witness observed a large flat object surrounded by dozens of smaller objects. Objects were observed nightly for nearly a month. On some occasions, witness was able to discern a low buzzing noise being emitted by the larger object. On one occasion, he reports that the object appeared to chase him along the boulevard.

July 1994. 9:30 P.M. Topanga Canyon State Park, Topanga Canyon. Dozens of witnesses including: the crew of *Encounters,* Preston Dennett, Dr. Steven Greer, Dr. Joseph Burkes and ten other members of the Los Angeles chapter of CSETI. Witnesses observe and film a large orange-white globe of light that rises above Henry Ridge.

July 16, 1994. 9:30 P.M. Topanga Canyon Boulevard near the Top o' Topanga, Topanga Canyon. Two witnesses: Bruce Merrifield and Reina Massey. Witnesses observed large solid object, hexagonal-shaped, covered with lights hover and move quickly away.

July 16, 1994. 9:30 P.M. Topanga Canyon State Park, Topanga Canyon. One witness: Preston Dennett. Witness observed a glowing bright light increase in diameter until it was the size of five full moons. The light winked out after about five seconds.

August 1994. 10:00–11:00 P.M. Topanga Canyon Boulevard near the Top o' Topanga, Topanga Canyon. Two witnesses: Phillip and Mandy. Witnesses observe a large globe of white light hovering low on the western horizon as they drive north out of the canyon and into the San Fernando Valley. Mandy observed an identical object on the second night. On the third night, the object failed to appear.

August 1994. 11:00 P.M. Old Topanga Canyon Road, Topanga Canyon. Two witnesses: Linda Jordan and her friend. Witnesses observed a large globe of white light hovering motionless low on the western horizon. After about fifteen minutes, the light disappeared.

November 1994. 11:30 P.M. Topanga Canyon Boulevard, Topanga Canyon. One witness: Mimi Smith. Witness was driving south along the boulevard when she saw a creature with densely packed white hair, a long neck, and holes where the eyes should be. Witness observed the creature about one month later in the same area.

So ends the list of encounters. Unfortunately, many could not be included because there was no date or no description of what was seen. Also, the list should by no means be considered comprehensive or complete. Without a doubt, this list represents only the tip of the iceberg of the actual number of accounts. As we have seen, there is reason to believe that the encounters number well into the thousands.

Although this list is incomplete, there are enough encounters to conduct a fairly accurate statistical analysis of the reports. The total number of reports is eighty-two.

The dates of the encounters range from 1942 to 1994. Two occurred in the 1940s. Two occurred in the 1950s. Two occurred in the 1960s. Fifteen occurred in the 1970s. Fourteen occurred in the 1980s. Forty-seven occurred in the 1990s.

The dates of the encounters shows an obvious trend of increasing UFO activity. Of course, this could also be explained in another way. It could be that the large numbers of encounters in the 1970s, '80s and '90s could be due to increased public awareness of UFOs. One puzzling aspect is the fact that the 1990s contain three times the number of encounters of any other decade. This may be because the Topanga Canyon UFO wave crested at that time. Interestingly, although I continue to get new accounts, the number of new accounts has decreased.

Whether these statistics show an increased level of UFO activity or an increasing public awareness of UFOs, the trend is in the same general direction;

UFOs are becoming more popular and encounters more frequent.

The times of the encounters show some interesting patterns. Unfortunately, most UFO witnesses are unable to remember the exact hour of their encounters, so I have divided the times into three general categories: Day (6:00 A.M.–6:00 P.M.); Evening (6:00 P.M.–12:00 midnight); Pre-Dawn (12:00 midnight–6:00 A.M.)

Eight of the encounters occurred during the day. Twenty-four of the encounters occurred during the pre-dawn hours. Forty-eight of the encounters occurred during the evening. Over sixty-five of the encounters occurred between the hours of 9:00 P.M. and 3:00 A.M. Statistically, those six hours are the best window in which to see a UFO. There were no encounters reported between the hours of 6:00 A.M. and 3:00 P.M. which would be statistically the rarest time to see a UFO. Two of the sightings spanned both the evening and pre-dawn hours.

The fact that no UFOs are reported during the morning and early afternoon hours would seem to indicate that the UFOs are simply not flying around. However, there are a significant number of high-quality daylight sightings. Why UFOs choose the evening to fly around would be pure speculation. Perhaps they feel they are less likely to be detected during the evening hours. And in fact, UFOs are probably most active during the pre-dawn hours; however, by that time, most people are asleep. If I were to recommend the best time to actually see a UFO over Topanga, I would say that the hours between midnight and 4:00 A.M. hold the best promise.

All but two of the incidents occurred in the Santa Monica Mountains. One incident occurred in Woodland Hills and one occurred in Beverly Hills, however, in both cases, the witnesses saw their UFOs over Topanga, and were technically in the foothills of the Santa Monica Mountains. The rest of the encounters are distributed between Topanga, Malibu, and Santa Monica. Topanga has the majority of encounters at forty-seven. Malibu has twenty-seven encounters. Santa Monica has six encounters.

The pattern is clear. Topanga is located entirely in the Santa Monica mountain range and therefore has the greatest number of reports. Most of Malibu is located within the Santa Monica mountain range, and has approximately two-thirds the number of encounters as Topanga. Only a small portion of Santa Monica is located within the Santa Monica mountain range, and as one would expect, only a small portion of the encounters come from Santa Monica. All the Santa Monica reports come from the mountainous regions, on the edge closest to Topanga. And as stated earlier, the Beverly Hills and Woodland Hills sightings both occurred within the foothills of the Santa Monica mountain range.

The focus of these sightings is obviously the Santa Monica Mountains. For whatever reason, it is extremely attractive to UFOs.

The location of the incidents within Topanga itself also show some interesting patterns. The great majority of encounters, twenty-six, took place in central Topanga Canyon, specifically within the State Park

282

area and along the boulevard between Old Topanga Canyon and Entrada. Eight of the encounters occurred on the southern edge of Topanga and up the Fernwood, Grandview, Saddlepeak area. Seven of the encounters occurred in the Old Canyon Road area. And six of the encounters occurred in north Topanga canyon, specifically within one mile of the Top o' Topanga overlook.

Again, the pattern shows that the greatest number of encounters is in the very heart of Topanga Canyon. However, each location has a representative sample of each type of encounter.

Five encounters actually took place over the ocean.

The number of witnesses of the eighty-two encounters totals at least one-hundred-thirty. I was able to conduct interviews with over fifty of the witnesses. At least fifteen of the witnesses have encountered UFOs on more than one occasion.

Many people believe that most UFO sightings occur only to single witnesses. In fact, nothing could be further from the truth. Only thirty-two of the eighty-two encounters involve only one witness. Thirty-eight encounters involve two witnesses. Six involve three witnesses. Two involve four witnesses. Two involve between five and ten witnesses. One involves between ten and twenty witnesses. And one case involves more than twenty witnesses.

The reason that so many UFOs are seen by groups of two people should be obvious; couples are the most common grouping of people. What is important here is that fifty of the encounters have more than one witness. The average number of witnesses per UFO encounter is 2.1.

The witnesses represent a typical cross-section of society. The ages of the witnesses vary from two years old to over sixty years old. The witnesses are evenly divided in sex and come from varying religious, educational and racial backgrounds. The occupations of the witnesses also vary widely. There are professionals including doctors, writers, teachers, military officers, pilots, and engineers. There are white-collar workers including computer programmers, nurses, therapists, secretaries. There are set designers, handymen, landscapers, photographers, students, managers, salespersons, homemakers, retirees, and at least one vagrant.

The only pattern among the witnesses is that there is no real pattern. The statistics show only that virtually anyone can see a UFO. One interesting factor is that many of the witnesses who report extensive encounters also exhibit some psychic ability or a deep interest in spirituality. Many of the witnesses had no prior knowledge of or interest in UFOs. Many were actually skeptical of the existence of UFOs, that is, until they had their own encounters. Of course, the Topanga Canyon UFO witnesses now believe in the existence of UFOs.

Of the eighty-two encounters, the most common type, at forty encounters, is anomalous lights. These include what are probably solid objects, but are so brightly lit that only lights can be discerned. These include lights that hover and dart at right angles. The appearance of the lights include star-like, oval-shaped, circular-shaped, flashes and beams.

Twenty-three of the cases involve what are obviously solid metallic craft, most of which had white lights or white and colored lights. The ships are variously described as shiny and metallic, dark-colored, and black; saucer-shaped, rectangular-shaped, hexagonal-shaped, bus-shaped, crystal-shaped, oddly-shaped.

There are six cases involving missing time and/or a possible onboard UFO experience.

Seven of the cases involve physical evidence in the form of crushed tree branches, circles of crushed vegetation, and physiological effects such as paralysis, loss of consciousness, nausea, pregnancy, and healing effects.

At least eight of the cases involve what appears to be some sort of telepathic communication between the witnesses and the UFOs.

Six of the cases involve beams of light being emitted from UFOs or from above. Nine of the cases involve objects that emit sounds which are described variously as buzzing, humming, and whooshing.

Six of the cases involve UFOs that chased people in their cars along the mountain roads.

Five of the cases involve some type of alien entity. The entities are described as either a presence, or a gray-type alien with a large hairless head, white skin, large black eyes, and short stature.

Three cases involve helicopters during the sighting.

Two cases involve UFOs that became transparent.

Two cases involve UFOs that floated above the ridges with the peculiar method of keeping an exact altitude, as if they had a height-governor, causing them to bob up and down in relation to the land formations.

Four cases show remarkable parallels. All occurred to woman who were dealing with various stages of pregnancy and childbirth. All involve repeated UFO visits. All involve telepathic communication with the objects. In the first case, a woman was pregnant with twins, but only one survived through childbirth. The witness feels the UFO was checking up on her pregnancy.

In the second case, the witness had a newborn baby only four days old when she experienced a UFO visitation two nights in a row.

In the third case, the witness became pregnant after her UFO encounter, and then experienced what is known as the missing-fetus syndrome. She was taught healing by the aliens.

In the fourth case, UFO abductee Kim Carlsberg reports seeing babies aboard a UFO.

Interestingly, in three of these cases, witnesses were told that there would be more earthquakes. In three of the cases, the witnesses noticed an increase in their intuitive abilities. Each of them was given information from the aliens.

There are other patterns. While most of the eighty-two UFO encounters were seen from the ground, two were seen from planes. At least a dozen cases occurred while people were driving.

The duration of the encounters varies from two seconds to four-and-a-half hours. Of those encounters which the duration of the sighting was known, at least twenty-four were under a minute in duration, twenty-six had a duration between one minute and one hour; and seven encounters endured for over an hour.

The total number of minutes logged seeing UFOs over Topanga is an astounding and approximate 1,342 minutes. That is a total of over eleven hours of sightings. The average duration of a sighting is about twenty-three minutes.

There are five cases of witnesses who saw the UFOs on two or more consecutive nights.

All this data makes several things clear. The encounters have been occurring for over fifty years. They can occur at any time, to any person, anywhere within the Santa Monica Mountains. Encounters of all types have occurred and are definitely on the increase.

The average Topanga Canyon UFO sighting or encounter involves 1.9 witnesses who see 4.5 darting star-like lights at around 11:00 P.M. for twenty-five minutes over the Topanga State Park area.

Notes

Chapter 6: They Return

1   In the Exeter, New Hampshire flap, investigator John Fuller uncovered evidence that the Air Force and FAA were investigating the sightings (Fuller, pp. 142-143, 166-170). In the Gulf Breeze, Florida flap, witnesses Ed and Frances Walters claimed to have been harrassed by the military (Walters, pp. 126-127). There were also numerous sightings of craft from apparent "unknown government agencies" in the Hudson Valley, NY UFO flap (Hynek, pp. 49-55). And in the Wytheville, Virginia sightings, lead investigator Danny Gordon became the victim of phone threats, possible government surveillance, and phone tapping. He was even invited to Langley AFB to discuss his investigations (Gordon, pp. 134-139, 152-153, 187). Obviously, these flap areas are not going completely unnoticed by the federal government.

Chapter 15: The Northridge Quake Encounters

2   Hopkins, Budd. *Witnessed*. 1996. pp. 356–398.

Chapter 18: Anatomy of a Cover-up

3   Wilkins, Harold T., *Flying Saucers on the Attack*. New York: Ace Books. 1954. pp. 284–289.

4   ibid. pg. 286.

5   Scully, Frank. *Behind the Flying Saucers*. New York: Henry Holt & Co., 1950. pp. 191–192.

6   Sword, Terrenz. *The Battle of Los Angeles, 1942*.

7   Rogo, D. Scott. *The Haunted Universe*. New American Library. New York, NY. 1977. pp. 120-121

8   Stanley, Robert. "UFOs over Malibu," *Unicus* magazine. Manhattan Beach, CA. Vol. 4, No. 1, 1995. pp. 16–17, 31.

9   Rogo, D. Scott (editor). *Alien Abductions: True Cases of UFO Kidnappings*. New York: New American Library. 1980. pg. 160.

10   See footnote #8.

Chapter 19: Why Topanga Canyon?

11   "*Children of the Rainbow,* by native Hawaiian Leinani Melville (Quest Books, 1969), is based on ancient oral traditions reserved for Hawaiian royalty. Melville was the first to introduce outsiders to this information: 'The original Hawaiians were of Hawaii (*Havai'i* or *Havai'ti,* "the streaming terrain over which moisture is rained") which originally referred to a very large island continent in the central Pacific Ocean. The first inhabitants of Havai'i were called the *Mu*. They migrated to Earth from *Ta'iti* (heaven), a place that was later confused (by Europeans) with a small island chain in the South Pacific. "From the

King of Heaven came the Mu. The spirit of his children flew hither in a gentle breeze that wafted from the Seven Divinities who surround the throne of God. They descend from his Holy Kingdom in a rainbow that flashed from the eternal realm of light. They came hither in a great river that flowed from the breast of heaven and poured from the King of Kings of the celestial spheres. They floated away from the regent of Heaven.'"

The Mayan *Torano Codex*, translated in 1896 by Augustus Le Plongeon, also states in part: 'The year 6 Kan, on the 11th Muluc, in the month Zac, there occurred a terrible earthquake, which continued without intermission until the 13th Chuen. The country of hills and mud, "The Land of Mu," was sacrificed. Being twice upheaved, it suddenly disappeared during the night, the basin being continually shaken by volcanic forces. At last the surface gave way, and the ten countries were torn asunder and scattered in fragments; unable to withstand the force of the seismic convulsions, they sank with their sixty-four million inhabitants, 8,060 years before the writing of this book.'

Le Plongeon's work was quoted extensively by Col. James Churchward in his series of books about Lemuria and the Mu. Churchward mentions that he had seen ancient historical records being preserved in Asia that related to the fate of the Mu." (correspondence from Robert Stanley, editor of *Unicus* magazine, February 1, 1999.)

Epilogue

12   Goldberg, Dr. Bruce. "Hypnotic Highways," *Fate* magazine, December, 1997. pp. 10-12.

Suggested Reading

Carlsberg, Kim. *Beyond My Wildest Dreams: Diary of A UFO Abductee*. Santa Fe, NM: Bear & Company. 1995.

Crystall, Ellen. *Silent Invasion: The Shocking Discoveries of a UFO Researcher*. New York: Paragon House. 1991.

Dennett, Preston. *One In Forty—The UFO Epidemic: True Accounts of Close Encounters With UFOs*. Commack, NY: Kroshka Books. 1996.

———. *UFO Healings: True Accounts of People Healed By Extraterrestrials*. Mill Spring, NC: Wild Flower Press. 1996.

Gordon, Danny B. and Paul Dellinger. *Don't Look Up! The Real Story Behind the Virginia UFO Sightings*. Madison, NC: Empire Publishing Inc. 1988.

Hopkins, Budd. *Missing Time: A Documented Study of UFO Abductions*. New York: Richard Marek Publishers. 1981.

———. *Witnessed: The True Story of the Brooklyn Bridge UFO Abductions*. New York: Pocket Books. 1996.

O'Brien, Christopher. *The Mysterious Valley*. New York: St. Martins Press. 1996.

Scully, Frank. *Behind the Flying Saucers*. New York: Henry Holt & Company. 1950.

Sword, Terrenz. *The Battle of Los Angeles, 1942*. Glendale, CA: Graven Images. 1992.

Walters, Ed and Frances Walters. *The Gulf Breeze Sightings: The Most Astounding Multiple Sightings of UFOs in U.S. History*. New York: William Morrow & Company, Inc. 1990.

———. *UFO Abductions in Gulf Breeze: The Amazing True Story of UFOs and the Real Visitors From Outer Space*. New York: Avon Books. 1994.

Wilkins, Harold T. *Flying Saucers on the Attack*. New York: Ace Books. 1954.

Index